TAKE YOUR MARK'S GOSPEL

BRIAN JOHNSTON

Copyright © 2018 HAYES PRESS. All rights reserved. No part of this book may be reproduced, stored in a retrieval system, or transmitted in any form, without the written permission of Hayes Press.

Published by:

HAYES PRESS CHRISTIAN RESOURCES

The Barn, Flaxlands

Royal Wootton Bassett

Swindon, SN4 8DY

United Kingdom

www.hayespress.org

e: info@hayespress.org

www.facebook.com/hayespress.org

http://twitter.com/hayespress

Unless otherwise indicated, all Scripture quotations are from the New American Standard Bible® (NASB®), Copyright © 1960, 1962, 1963, 1968, 1971, 1972, 1973, 1975, 1977, 1995 by The Lockman Foundation. Used by permission (www.Lockman.org).

CONTENTS

CHAPTER ONE: JOINING THE DOTS

CHAPTER TWO: JESUS CAN DEMAND ALLEGIANCE

CHAPTER THREE: THE IMPACT OF JESUS' TEACHING

CHAPTER FOUR: HOW TO LISTEN WELL AND GAIN INSIGHT

CHAPTER FIVE: THE HEART OF THE PROBLEM: SYMPTOMS, DIAGNOSIS AND CURE

CHAPTER SIX: THE CHANGING OF AN ERA / MOVING INTO GENTILE TERRITORY

CHAPTER SEVEN: GAINING INSIGHT AT LAST

CHAPTER EIGHT: SEEING HALF THE PICTURE

CHAPTER NINE: LOSING LIFE, DENYING SELF AND BECOMING LITTLE

CHAPTER TEN: SAVIOUR OR JUDGE?

CHAPTER ELEVEN: VARIOUS CONFLICTS IN THE TEMPLE COURTS

CHAPTER TWELVE: THE END OF THE TEMPLE AND MUCH MORE

CHAPTER THIRTEEN: RECLINING AT TABLE

CHAPTER FOURTEEN: BETRAYED, DENIED AND VERY ALONE

CHAPTER FIFTEEN: THE KING WHO STUMBLED TO HIS THRONE

CHAPTER SIXTEEN: THE MOST IMPORTANT PRESS RELEASE IN HISTORY

CHAPTER ONE: JOINING THE DOTS

So you want to do some Bible study? Are you ready? All set? Then take your Mark's Gospel ... and let's begin. As I begin, I'm thinking of those puzzle pictures I used to create as a child. You know the type you get in a printed book. Printed on the page are nothing but black dots, but they're far from randomly positioned – although at first they convey no meaning whatsoever. Beside each small dot, however, there's a number. I still recall the childish enjoyment of taking a pen and then carefully joining the dots in the numbered sequence. Very soon you saw the pattern of dots transform into the picture of something, perhaps an elephant. Due to other bold lines that were also there to represent trees, etc., it had not been obvious from the beginning this was how it was going to turn out.

I once heard about how such dot-to-dot exercises were handed out to keep two children quiet at a church service. One child dutifully joined the dots in number order and they formed a simple 'boxy' cross shape within a square grid array of dots. The other child was much more imaginative, however, and basically ignored the dots and drew a free hand picture of some flowers all over them. To be fair it did look more interesting, but it was not the intended meaning.

Unfortunately, it's possible to read the Bible in something resembling each of these two ways: either by following the contextual clues that are God-given or else by superimposing our own creative imagination in some fanciful way of interpreting the Bible text. Hopefully, as we turn now to Mark's Gospel, we'll succeed in confining ourselves to reading the intended meaning out from the text, and not superimpose our own creative notions.

But first, another illustration, if I may. Some of you may remember a television detective series, once popular in the United States. The central character was a quirky figure who went by the name of Columbo. Usually, in this genre of viewing material – that is, of murder mysteries – the way the producer keeps viewers intrigued is to withhold vital additional information until almost the last moment. When it finally surfaces, the on-screen detective -and we, the viewers at home – are able to solve the crime in a previously quite unexpected way. But with the Columbo series, it was different. The viewers were let in on what had actually happened right at the beginning. The viewers' interest was all about watching the on-screen detective stumble his way towards solving it; perhaps, a little like when you hide something for your young children to find. They enjoy trying to find it, and you enjoy watching them get ever closer by trial and error.

How is the Gospel by Mark like this? Well, right at the beginning, we read: *"The beginning of the gospel of Jesus Christ, the Son of God"* (Mark 1:1). Those are the words of the first verse with which it opens. Mark's Gospel doesn't build its way up to this momentous disclosure after first presenting all the circumstantial evidence. No, Mark comes right out with it, and then proceeds to defend and justify the claim by arranging his account of Jesus' life on earth in such a way that it offers supporting evidence for this dramatic opening claim that Jesus Christ is the son of God.

Now compare that with say, the Gospel by John. It's only when we reach the twentieth chapter of John's Gospel and verse 31, that we read that it was written so that we might believe that Jesus is the son of God, and that by believing we might have life in his name. John's Gospel builds towards this emphatic confirmation of what all the recorded signs had been leading the reader towards: that Jesus is God's son.

Not only does Mark open his Gospel with such a plain statement of what it's all about, by identifying right at the outset who Jesus Christ is, but this is, in fact, the first of three similar confessions that are to be found in the Gospel. The first is right at the very beginning, as we've said. The second, in the middle of it, comes from the lips of Peter, and so we can refer to it as Peter's confession, when he said to Jesus, *"You are the Christ, the Son of the living God."* And finally, the third confession is very close to the end of the Gospel, and is found in the story of the crucifixion. There, at the foot of the cross, and seeing Jesus die, the centurion cries out: *"Truly this man was the son of God."*

Those 3 confessions (Mark 1:1; Mark 8:29; Mark 15:39) give a sort of beginning, middle and ending structure to Mark's gospel, with the central confession in some sense acting like a hinge between focusing on the 'who?' question – that is, who Jesus is - before majoring afterwards on the 'why?' question – that is, why did Jesus die? Those are the two most important questions that can engage the human mind, which makes Mark's Gospel essential reading for us all.

But with that taster and brief introductory guide, let's rewind back to the beginning again, and start with Mark at chapter one, verse one – with that first confession that gives the game away right at the outset.

By the way, in Mark 1:1 the word 'gospel' simply means 'good news'. And with Mark's opening declaration that Jesus Christ is God's son, what Mark is at once telling us is this: that the good news is a person! Usually good news is when something happens. But the best news for the human race was when this person came. God had been promising this would happen for thousands of years, and Mark recalls that Isaiah the prophet, in particular, had spoken about him (Mark 1:2,3). In the Old Testament, God had promised his people, who at that time were the nation of Israel, a Messiah (that is, someone anointed, as kings were, to deliver all who follow him from their dread predicament). They'd waited for many hundreds of years. Now, at last, Jesus himself announces: *"The time has come"* (Mark 1:15). In other words, Jesus is being introduced as the King of God's kingdom: he'll be the one to rule over God's people. Another point to be clear on is this: that 'Christ' is not really just another part of Jesus' name. It's his office or job title. Jesus was the 'Christ' or king that God sent.

Jesus is God's son. It's official. God says so. Jesus has come to tell the good news: that God's kingdom is arriving. The only appropriate response is that we should believe it and turn away from our sins (which is what the word 'repent' means, as used by Mark when he reports on what Jesus' initial preaching was about). He told – in fact, he commanded - people to repent. It was time for Jesus to begin his work. His work was to bring the good news, to announce that the time for God's kingdom had finally arrived.

But where does the action begin? The report cuts away to a river scene in verse nine (Mark 1:9), the same river that had been the butt of a famous put-down in the Old Testament (2 Kings 5). Jesus' public ministry starts from there – down by the Jordan, "The Jordan" being the name of the river in which John the Baptist had previously – up until this moment – been baptizing people.

And what's the very first thing Jesus did (Mark 1:9)? He allowed himself to be 'baptised' (or put under the water) by his relative John, who was God's Messenger. The Messenger, John, has now completed his preparing of the ground for the Messiah, Jesus. And so the spotlight switches to Jesus' life and ministry, and away from John's.

Up until now, John has been telling the people how special Jesus is (Mark 1:4-8). Now God himself takes over, and speaks from heaven! John had been right about Jesus. As Jesus emerged from the water of the river Jordan, a voice coming from heaven declared, *"You are my beloved Son, in You I am well-pleased"* (Mark 1:11). This is the ultimate commendation, from God the Father himself. Elsewhere in the Bible, we read that God looks down from heaven to earth, and says, *"There is none who does good"* (Romans 3:12). Jesus Christ is unique. The only hope for this world is found in him. There's no good news in any human self-help scheme. Nor in any religious tradition. There's but one name given under heaven by which we can be saved from divine judgement to come, and that's the name of Jesus (Acts 4:12).

Malcolm Muggeridge came to recognize this, and say: "In one lifetime I have seen my own fellow countrymen ruling over a quarter of the world ... I've heard a crazed, cracked Austrian proclaim to the world the establishment of a German Reich that would last a thousand years; an Italian clown announce that he would restart the calendar to begin with his own assumption of power. I've heard a murderous Georgian brigand in the Kremlin acclaimed by the intellectual elite of the world as a wiser than Solomon ... All in one little lifetime. All gone with the wind. ... Hitler and Mussolini dead, remembered only in infamy. Stalin a forbidden name in the regime he helped found and dominate for some three decades ... All in one lifetime, all gone. Gone with the wind. Behind the debris of these self-styled, sullen supermen and imperial diplomatists, there stands the gigantic figure of one person, because of whom, by whom, in whom, and through whom alone mankind might still have hope - the person of Jesus Christ."

Well, as we've said, God was pleased to announce the public start of his son's earthly mission, but Satan (that's the Devil) was angry. Satan wanted to stop Jesus. He tried to stop the good news spreading. Satan tempted Jesus to try, if it was possible, to have him follow an easier path, easier than the one his Father had planned for him. But Jesus didn't listen to Satan, God's adversary. This seems to hint at a contrast with God's people, Israel, in the desert (recorded in the books of Exodus and Numbers) fifteen hundred years earlier. They'd failed their test. Israel chose not to trust God. But Jesus didn't fail his test.

For forty days, a day for every year of Israel's big test in the desert, Jesus was in the desert being tested (Mark 1:13).

Jesus passes the test, and comes out of the desert to preach the good news. John cannot preach the good news any longer because he's been imprisoned (Mark 1:14). Now, Jesus tells people the same message that John did, but adds much more information. The fullest disclosure we have about God, our maker and judge, comes through Jesus Christ, and Mark's Gospel, which we've only begun to study, has so much more to tell us.

Isn't it great when a queue we've been waiting in starts moving at last? The good news is that people do not have to wait any longer. The king has come. The person who can forgive their sins has come. But what that now means is that it's time for us to do something.

For further discussion:

1. Have you any comments on the style and substance of Mark's story-telling?
2. What impression of the coming kingdom is being given?
3. Other than through the life of Jesus, in what other ways can we get to know something about God?
4. What kind of response is being called for from us?

CHAPTER TWO: JESUS CAN DEMAND ALLEGIANCE

Mark has told us that Jesus is the Christ, the son of God. John the Baptist had laid the groundwork, telling all who would listen that Jesus would soon come. None less than God himself has told us that Jesus is his son. The special someone whom people had been waiting for had finally arrived (Mark 1:1-15).

But like those people back then, we're also naturally sceptical. And often with good reason in a world of broken promises and false dawns. Why should we believe what Mark is telling us about Jesus? If he truly is God's Son, the long-awaited King to come and deliver us from the sad state of affairs in this world with its litany of human pain and suffering, then we'd expect the life he should live to be utterly special. A life without any peer. Mark sets out to demonstrate that it was.

People often ask the question: 'I wonder what heaven will be like?' Another similar question is: 'What will God's future kingdom be like?' In Jesus' earthly life, it's as if we get a tester-pot of kingdom colours. You know what I mean by a tester point, don't you? One day, you decide to give your paintwork at home a refresh. You want to redecorate, but there's a snag - you haven't held onto the old paint tin. When you visit the paint shop again, there are two shades of paint that seem very close to what you already have. But which is it? The shop assistant solves the problem by giving you a small tester pot of each colour. You can now go home and on a small area of the wall you can apply a little paint from each tester pot. You observe one to be the correct shade, and so you go back confidently now to buy a large tin of that shade of paint you now know to be the correct one. In a similar way, perhaps, we can think about the three years of Jesus' public life of service in this world as a tester pot, showing us the true colours of what life will be like in God's kingdom to come, as in the prayer he taught his followers: 'your kingdom come, your will be done.'

But perhaps your mind is racing ahead at this point, because you already know something about how the story of Jesus' life on earth ends. His death is surely the most famous in history, after all. But, the point is, if Mark's opening confession is true, why on earth did Jesus have to die on a cross? How can that be consistent with a foretaste of the kingdom to come? Mark's Gospel is going to help us discover that Jesus had to die so that we might be able to have a place in that coming kingdom. Of course, we'd rather focus on the miracles of Jesus' life than on his gruesome death, but let's join the dots of the picture as Mark intends.

At this point, I'm reminded of when my mother-in-law mentioned that she'd mice in her house. She spoke of cleaning up their droppings. Well, as we know, that solves the immediate problem, but soon there'll be more! Her daughter then reminded her that there was a mouse-trap in the cupboard. Soon that was set up and it did its job of trapping the mouse. That was the end of the story. The problem had now been dealt with at source - at the level of the root cause – and not simply dealing with the symptoms.

Jesus' life was full of dealing with the symptoms of humanity's original sin. Practically everywhere he went, he dispensed healing and blessing, bringing great joy into the lives of so many people. But later these same people would get ill again and eventually die. The problem of the human condition goes a whole lot deeper. To deal with the root problem of the human condition, Jesus needed to go to the cross and die. But more about that later.

What we find Jesus doing almost as soon as he began calling on people to turn back to God, was to enlist the help of others to be his followers, to be his disciples, in particular the group that came to be known as 'the Twelve.' They, and so many others, would be the ones to carry on spreading God's good news, the story of God's remedy for human sin, after Jesus had returned to heaven.

It's this enlisting of his first followers that first begins to show us the kind of authority we'd expect a king to have. We should read about this for ourselves directly from Mark chapter 1:

> *"Now after John had been taken into custody, Jesus came into Galilee, preaching the gospel of God, and saying, "The time is fulfilled, and the kingdom of God is at hand; repent and believe in the gospel." As He was going along by the Sea of Galilee, He saw Simon and Andrew, the brother of Simon, casting a net in the sea; for they were fishermen. And Jesus said to them, "Follow Me, and I will make you become fishers of men." Immediately they left their nets and followed Him. Going on a little farther, He saw James the son*

of Zebedee, and John his brother, who were also in the boat mending the nets. Immediately He called them; and they left their father Zebedee in the boat with the hired servants, and went away to follow Him" (Mark 1:14-20).

Whoa, let's stop and take that on board. Imagine you see someone who is busy at work. He has a good job. He has a house and a family to look after. Suppose you were to go up to him and tell him to leave his work and follow you without offering to pay him any money. What will he tell you to do? I think the expression these days is: 'On yer bike, mate!' But when Jesus says: 'Follow me!', what happens? They drop everything and start to follow!

That shows us something awesome about Jesus' power. That's the point of mentioning this here straight after the Gospel's opening claims about Jesus. In this section of Mark's gospel, we have an example of Jesus' royal authority in the power that he has over some fishermen. These men became special followers of Jesus. We call them his disciples. Jesus, God's Son, also has the power to tell us what to do. By the way, as the name suggests, the 'Sea of Galilee' is a small lake in the area of Galilee. Most people have heard of Simon, the first mentioned of Jesus' disciples – if not by that name, then by his other name, Peter. It was Jesus who gave Simon the name 'Peter'. Simon (Peter), Andrew, James and John were 4 of the 12 disciples of Jesus.

I think we should pause and emphasize Mark's point here: why he arranges his material this way. Remember, he's begun with the stunning claim that Jesus is God's son, the promised king.

That's a truth claim - how can it be verified? We need to evaluate it by checking if there's evidence consistent with it. In other words, the big issue Mark focuses our attention on is this: does Jesus display the kind of authority that's expected from a king?

We're going to discover that Mark will now present one piece of evidence after another to convince us that Jesus does have the authority of heaven's king while here on earth. The first example of the use of his authority is seen in calling these fishermen to be his followers. These were grown men, with families, and a business. They'd been brought up to a life of fishing. They probably knew nothing else. Their horizons were very limited. They – and everyone else – expected them to follow their fathers in the family fishing business. That's what you did in those times. If your father was a fisherman or a baker or a carpenter, then you learned from him the trade of being a fisherman or baker or carpenter. And that was that – so different from today, at least in western lands.

It's easy for us to miss this point. But even the calling of those fishermen was in a sense miraculous, certainly a wonder. The point wasn't lost on the great French general, Napoleon. At a point, later in his life, while in exile with time to reflect on ultimate issues, he had this to say while talking with his colleagues.

'Christ alone succeeded in so raising the mind of man toward the unseen that it became insensible to the barrier of time and space. Across a chasm of 1,800 years, Jesus Christ made a demand which is beyond all others difficult to satisfy ... [Jesus] asks for the human heart. He demands it unconditionally and forthwith his demand is granted. Wonderful! In defiance of time and space, the spirit of man with all its powers and faculties becomes an annexation to the empire of Christ. All who sincerely believe experience that supernatural love towards him.' Napoleon commented further, 'this phenomenon is unaccountable,' and said it was this that showed convincingly to him the divinity of Jesus Christ. Notice it was in this authority – in the calling and commanding of followers – that Napoleon discerned the royal dignity of Christ, the ruler of a kingdom infinitely greater than any empire he'd built up.

So, getting back to the shoreline of the sea of Galilee, what did Simon and Andrew and James and John do when Jesus told them to follow him (Mark 1:18)? Jesus had a special job for these men. Jesus doesn't want everyone to stop doing their usual job. He doesn't call everyone to be preachers. Before, they caught fish; now, they must 'catch' people. Jesus will teach them to tell people the good news about him. Then some will come into his 'net', and be included in his kingdom.

These men 'left all' - the familiarity and security of home and occupation. They simply sensed he was worth it; a decision based on kingdom values. These men left their small-town ambitions for kingdom-building. They were hard at work when Jesus called them, but they were called to harder work still.

When Christ calls, don't say, 'I can't' for Christ says, 'I will make you.' It's not about us; it's all about him.

For discussion:

1. Sceptics may cite a lack of evidence for us to believe in Jesus, how would you answer this based on our reading of Mark to date?
2. What is the most significant feature of the background to Jesus' choosing of the Twelve?
3. C.S. Lewis once spoke about the destiny of the person who rejects Christ as being about how God respects their choice. Do you agree with this? Does it gain any support from Mark?
4. Jesus doesn't chase after the crowds with their shallow interest, but drew to himself those expressing deeper interest. Are we getting the balance right?

CHAPTER THREE: THE IMPACT OF JESUS' TEACHING

The question that was asked was: 'What was the greatest speech ... ever given?' The person answering was Robert Schlesinger, managing editor for opinion at U.S. News & World Report. This is what he said: 'Most people who know me – and know that at best I'm agnostic – might be surprised by my answer. For sheer reach and influence, it's hard to argue against Jesus' Sermon on the Mount. It comes down to how you define 'greatest.' I chose to interpret it in terms of the breadth of the effect it's had through history. It's hard to beat ... whether or not you believe he was divine, the son of the Nazarene carpenter is one of the most influential figures in history.'

In this study, we'll be considering the impact of Jesus' teaching. There's not a whole lot of teaching by Jesus recorded for us in Mark's Gospel – certainly not compared to the five major blocks of recorded teaching we find in Matthew's Gospel. Mark's record of Jesus life and ministry is short on talk and long on action – with that action repeatedly being characterized as decisive and effective. Watch out everywhere throughout this Gospel for Mark's use of the word 'immediately' or 'straightway.' But let's begin by picking up on Robert Schlesinger's hesitation over the divinity or deity of Jesus of Nazareth. We've previously observed that Napoleon had no such hesitation. And it was typically black and white for the

TAKE YOUR MARK'S GOSPEL

sharp mind of Oxford and Cambridge scholar and author C.S. Lewis.

He said there were only three possible choices. Jesus is Lord, liar, or lunatic. There are no other options, such as he was only a good man and a good teacher but nothing more than that! His argument went something like this. Jesus claims he is the son of God (see Mark 14:62). If that's true, then that's who he is. If it's false and he knew it was false, then that makes him a liar. On the other hand, if it's false and he didn't know it was, then that makes him a lunatic.

The Gospel by Mark is defending Lewis' first option: that the claim that Jesus is the son of God is the correct one. The whole Gospel is written to support that awesome claim. The life described so fully and beautifully in its pages is the most wonderful life the planet has seen. It is most decidedly not the life of a conman or a deranged individual. As we've seen, Mark supports the claim that Jesus is Lord by giving us example after example of Jesus' authority following on from the stunning opening claim that Jesus is the son of God. We've already begun to track some of these, starting with the authority by which he could command the allegiance of his followers (Mark 1:16-20 and even now). That's now followed by a demonstration of his authority to teach (Mark 1:21-28). We'll let Mark take up the story of Jesus' life:

> *"They went into Capernaum; and immediately on the Sabbath He entered the synagogue and began to teach. They were amazed at His teaching; for He was teaching them as one having authority, and not as the*

> *scribes. Just then there was a man in their synagogue with an unclean spirit; and he cried out, saying, "What business do we have with each other, Jesus of Nazareth? Have You come to destroy us? I know who You are—the Holy One of God!" And Jesus rebuked him, saying, "Be quiet, and come out of him!" Throwing him into convulsions, the unclean spirit cried out with a loud voice and came out of him. They were all amazed, so that they debated among themselves, saying, "What is this? A new teaching with authority! He commands even the unclean spirits, and they obey Him"* (Mark 1:21-27).

Those who heard Jesus teach were clearly impressed. They were amazed at the authority that came through in his teaching. It was so unlike all the teaching they were used to, which was the teaching of the Jewish scribes.

How was Jesus unlike the scribes? Later, in his public ministry, Jesus himself would say: *"Every scribe who has become a disciple of the kingdom of heaven is like a head of a household, who brings out of his treasure things new and old"* (Matthew 13:52). Commenting on this, one Bible expert says: "The mere scribe, Rabbinical in spirit, produces only the old and stale. The disciple of the kingdom like the Master, is always fresh-minded, yet knows how to value all old spiritual treasures of Holy Writ ..." (F. F. Bruce).

In what sense was Jesus' teaching 'new' (v.27)? In the sense of the freshness of its quality. Bible teaching wasn't new to these Jewish audiences, from the time of Ezra the scribe others had done that. But Jesus was not merely repeating, he was speaking with the authority of the Author!

But there's more. For as Jesus was speaking, he was challenged. This was way beyond the kind of heckling a speaker might occasionally encounter if what he says is thought-provoking. It came from a member of the audience whose life and whole being was possessed by an unclean, that is an evil, spirit. In the Jewish religion of the time, obsessed as it was with ritual cleanliness and ceremonial cleansings, it's ironic to think of how in their midst in their Jewish church assembly or synagogue, here was such evident uncleanness. Surely the powerlessness of their religious tradition was being contrasted here by Mark with the power of Jesus. The exorcism by Jesus that followed was to illustrate the power of his teaching, and to give a definite clue as to the identity of the one who was teaching that day.

The demon spoke for all of its dark realm ('us') – it had no difficulty identifying the Lord, in stark contrast to the humans present, which is a further irony.

So, to commanding allegiance (Mark 1:16-20); and to teaching (Mark 1:21-28); healing – or rather, exorcism - is now added (Mark 1:29-45) as the next example of God-like authority. Remember, this is Mark's apologetic, his defence, for Jesus as the divine son of God. It's sometimes said that Jesus never claimed to be God. I want you to consider if that's an accurate assessment, based on how the second chapter of Mark's Gospel opens:

"When He had come back to Capernaum several days afterward, it was heard that He was at home. And many were gathered together, so that there was no longer room, not even near the door; and He was speaking the word to them. And they came, bringing to Him a paralytic, carried by four men. Being unable to get to Him because of the crowd, they removed the roof above Him; and when they had dug an opening, they let down the pallet on which the paralytic was lying. And Jesus seeing their faith said to the paralytic, "Son, your sins are forgiven." But some of the scribes were sitting there and reasoning in their hearts, "Why does this man speak that way? He is blaspheming; who can forgive sins but God alone?"

Immediately Jesus, aware in His spirit that they were reasoning that way within themselves, said to them, "Why are you reasoning about these things in your hearts? "Which is easier, to say to the paralytic, 'Your sins are forgiven'; or to say, 'Get up, and pick up your pallet and walk'? "But so that you may know that the Son of Man has authority on earth to forgive sins" - He said to the paralytic, "I say to you, get up, pick up your pallet and go home." And he got up and immediately picked up the pallet and went out in the sight of everyone, so that they were all amazed and were glorifying God, saying, "We have never seen anything like this" (Mark 2:1-12).

Surely there could not have been a more emphatic way for Jesus to press his claim to be fully God as well as fully human. He affirmed only God can forgive sins – then proceeded to do so! We need to know our sins forgiven, just like this man, so we too can have a relationship with God.

Early in Mark's Gospel, Jesus invokes the imagery of a wedding. People love weddings. It's amazingly reassuring to discover that God also wants a relationship with us!

> *"John's disciples and the Pharisees were fasting; and they came and said to Him, "Why do John's disciples and the disciples of the Pharisees fast, but Your disciples do not fast?" And Jesus said to them, "While the bridegroom is with them, the attendants of the bridegroom cannot fast, can they? So long as they have the bridegroom with them, they cannot fast. But the days will come when the bridegroom is taken away from them, and then they will fast in that day. No one sews a patch of unshrunk cloth on an old garment; otherwise the patch pulls away from it, the new from the old, and a worse tear results. No one puts new wine into old wineskins; otherwise the wine will burst the skins, and the wine is lost and the skins as well; but one puts new wine into fresh wineskins"* (Mark 2:18-22).

Weddings, of course, are all about happiness, not mourning! How inappropriate it would have been for Jesus' disciples to fast while their Lord was still with them! And from the illustration about the patches on wineskins, we learn the need for totally new thinking. Fermenting wine as it produces gas demands flexibility in the completely new skin that contains it. *"My thoughts are not your thoughts"* (God says in Isaiah 55:8). Jesus didn't come to bolster human religious tradition. Jesus brought something new their previous religious tradition couldn't contain. There is an acknowledgement here of the difficulty in teaching people who have long-held and fixed ideas: "the old is good enough," they say. Jesus came to call us to repentance, to a change of mind, to God's fresh and true teaching. May I ask: 'Is the Bible now speaking freshly to you?'

For discussion:

1. In the Old Testament, disease was at times viewed as the consequence of someone's (specific) sin, and healing was based on God's forgiveness (e.g., Numbers 12:10; 2 Chronicles 16:12; 26:19). Does Jesus imply here that this man's physical condition had a direct spiritual cause?
2. Compare the determination of the five characters who come to Jesus here with the stubborn resistance of Saul of Tarsus. How can we accommodate such differences as we witness to others?
3. Only God can forgive sins (cf. Exodus 34:6-9; Psalm 103:3; 130:4; Isaiah 43:25; Isaiah 44:22; Isaiah 48:11; Daniel 9:9). In the Old Testament forgiveness of sins was never attributed to the Messiah. Were the Jews expecting a Messiah who was divine, or not?
4. Jesus confronted them with counter-questions (which was the way the Rabbis debated cf. Mark 3:4; Mark 11:30; Mark 12:37). Why do you think he did this, rather than simply acting?
5. Jesus commanded the paralytic to 1) get up, and then 2) to take his mat, and go home. Do you see a different intention behind these two requests? (Compare Mark 1:45).
6. Does this in any way reflect the extent of the salvation Jesus was bringing as ultimately being the healing of the whole person (body and soul)?

CHAPTER FOUR: HOW TO LISTEN WELL AND GAIN INSIGHT

You watch and enjoy a football match. You cheer when your team scores a goal and talk about the match afterwards - but the match doesn't change you! In the same way, perhaps, you come to church, open your Bible, and enjoy the service. You sing the hymns and even talk about the sermon - but does it change you? This study invites us to check out how we listen to God.

In Mark's presentation of how Jesus selected people and gave authoritative answers, we arrive next at one of Jesus' most famous parables. It's in chapter 4, and, as we've hinted, it's a parable all about listening. Some folks think Jesus told parables to make it easy for people to understand about God. But can that be the full story? Listen to Jesus:

> *"As he was sowing, some seed fell beside the road, and the birds came and ate it up. Other seed fell on the rocky ground where it did not have much soil; and immediately it sprang up because it had no depth of soil. And after the sun had risen, it was scorched; and because it had no root, it withered away. Other seed fell among the thorns, and the thorns came up and choked it, and it yielded no crop. Other seeds fell into the good soil, and as they grew up and increased, they yielded*

> *a crop and produced thirty, sixty, and a hundredfold"* (Mark 4:3-8).

Now, let me ask you: 'What does that tell you about God?' That's not so easy to answer, is it? To get a clue that this is a parable or story about how to listen to God, let's rewind to its introduction, as given by Mark. Always remember as we do Bible study that context is most important.

> *"He began to teach again by the sea. And such a very large crowd gathered to Him that He got into a boat in the sea and sat down; and the whole crowd was by the sea on the land. And He was teaching them many things in parables, and was saying to them in His teaching, "Listen to this! Behold, the sower went out to sow ..." And He was saying, "He who has ears to hear, let him hear"* (Mark 4:1-3,9)

> *"As soon as He was alone, His followers, along with the twelve, began asking Him about the parables. And He was saying to them, "To you has been given the mystery of the kingdom of God, but those who are outside get everything in parables, so that WHILE SEEING, THEY MAY SEE AND NOT PERCEIVE, AND WHILE HEARING, THEY MAY HEAR AND NOT UNDERSTAND, OTHERWISE THEY MIGHT RETURN AND BE FORGIVEN"* (Mark 4:10-12).

In those verses, there are two groups of people (in vv.10-12): first, people who turn away from Jesus ('those who are outside'); second, people who believe in Jesus ('His followers, along with the Twelve'). Jesus teaches his disciples and the people who'll listen to him. The outsiders wouldn't have him as king, so Jesus doesn't let them in on his teaching.

"He who has ears to hear, let him hear" (Mark 4:9). These words of Jesus are the key to unlock his teaching in this story. It's about how we listen to God's Word. At the end, Jesus tells us to be careful how we listen. And He was saying, *"He who has ears to hear, let him hear."* We all have ears ... but are they 'ears to hear'?

Jesus' parables judge the people who should have welcomed their Messiah. But they had hard hearts, refusing to listen. So, Jesus judges them by not teaching in a direct way, but in parables which they'll not understand well. Jesus' words either change us or judge us. Listening is our responsibility.

> *"And He was saying to them, "A lamp is not brought to be put under a basket, is it, or under a bed? Is it not brought to be put on the lampstand? For nothing is hidden, except to be revealed; nor has anything been secret, but that it would come to light. If anyone has ears to hear, let him hear." And He was saying to them, "Take care what you listen to. By your standard of measure it will be measured to you; and more will be given you besides. For whoever has, to him more shall be given; and whoever does not have, even what he has shall be taken away from him"* (Mark 4:21-25).

TAKE YOUR MARK'S GOSPEL   29

In other words, listeners or insiders are not to be kept in the dark permanently. If we have a serious listening ear, then more understanding will be given (v.24). That's good to know, isn't it? Let's apply that now, as we try to listen to the message that begins at the end of this fourth chapter and extends through chapter five also. The repetition ought to get our attention. Four stories are presented, each on the heels of the other. The calming of the storm (Mark 4:35-41); the exorcism of 'Legion' (Mark 5:1-20); the healing of a woman with a haemorrhage; and the raising of Jairus' daughter (Mark 5:21-43). This quick succession drives home the point to true listeners: and the point is that Jesus is the best person to turn to in a crisis.

Jesus had shown in the first place that even the wind and the sea obey him (Mark 4:41). His authority extends to the natural realm as well as the spiritual and human. He'd then tamed the man possessed with a legion or multitude of evil spirits, a man whom previously no-one had been able to bind (Mark 5:4). The woman whose bleeding he stopped when she made contact by reaching out in faith and touching the hem of his cloak - she was someone who had spent all her living, endured a lot in being treated by many doctors, but hadn't been helped at all. Jesus ended her twelve-year search for a cure.

She came in a crowd, but her encounter with Jesus would end up as personal. There was no special healing property in Jesus' cloak, but she accessed Jesus' own virtue by means of stooping down and reaching out in faith to him. And in the fourth story, he turned mournful wailing into astounding joy. The outstanding faith of Jairus, the synagogue official, is again key to the blessing received. All of these short cameos present the same message: Jesus is mighty to save. He's the best person to turn to in any kind of crisis.

Sadly, however, Jesus' followers – including the Twelve – were not always the best listeners, and so they were slow to get the point. Mark now makes a striking contrast with two individuals whom we encounter in these four stories. We have a saying about waiting for a bus, and it's takes a very long time to come; and suddenly, two come at once! I'm reminded of that when I think about these two people: the woman with the haemorrhage and the synagogue official, the father of the daughter who'd died. Until now, as we've been following Mark, there's been little evidence of people with faith in Jesus. Jesus has even had to question why the disciples don't trust him. Now, surely by design, Mark puts these two stories together. They each teach the same lesson. And that lesson is that we, too, need to act in real faith not just with a casual assent to the facts.

Mark then mentions a visit Jesus made to his hometown of Nazareth where he wondered at their unbelief. This is typically the only thing Jesus is said to have 'wondered at' during his life on earth: he wondered at the lack of faith on the part of those who'd been privileged to have some of the best seats in the house. Mark tells us Jesus *"could do no miracle there except that He laid His hands on a few sick people and healed them"* (Mark 6:5). It would be easy to misunderstand this statement. There's nothing impossible for the Lord; the sense is he chose not to work miracles due to the unbelief he encountered there. The same wording is used for the refusal of those who, in one of Jesus' stories, were invited to a wedding banquet, but replied that they had just got married and so 'could not' come. Again, not a physical impossibility, but a matter of choice.

We mentioned facts that ought to have given rise to faith. But what evidence really ought to have stimulated the disciples' faith? At this point in the Gospel, we have two back-to-back miracles. The first is perhaps the most famous of all Jesus' miracles: it's the feeding of the five thousand. Here were 5,000 reasons to believe that Jesus can satisfy the spiritual hunger in each human heart. But right afterwards, Jesus walks on water to still the waves of the sea – surely also with the intention to still the waves of doubt in his followers' hearts.

However, the response of the disciples is emphasized as being particularly disappointing (Mark 6:52). They're criticised for failing to gain insight through these miracles: specifically, the two miracles of feeding the five thousand and Jesus' walking to them on the sea.

Is there something more than meets the eye here? In the Old Testament, in the history of God's people, Israel, we find two major historic miracles involving walking across a sea and eating bread in a desert place. Does Mark intend us to recall these, by virtue of him placing these two miracles of a sea-crossing and a desert feeding side by side? We can at least ask the questions: 'Were these miracles of deliverance at sea and feeding in a desert intentionally related by placing them side by side in Mark's Gospel?' 'Were they meant to trigger in them the realization that a greater redemption was now underway?' Greater, that is, than the escape from the land of Egypt with its slavery.

If so – and it cannot be expressed more strongly than that – then all we can say is that Jesus' disciples failed to see the possible bigger picture. They gained no insight from the miracle(s), Mark tells us, as their mind was closed (Mark 6:52). Let's try to do better. Let's try to read not only this Gospel, but the whole Bible in context, and aim at getting the big picture. Remember, observing and listening well, and gaining insight, is something the Lord holds us responsible to do. It applies no less today than back them. The Twelve had begun so well. They'd responded promptly to the Lord's authority when he called them. They'd left all and followed him. That was stunning. Now, it's not so impressive. Later (Mark 8:17), the Lord will directly challenge these disciples if they have closed minds, minds that fail to grasp the insight they ought to be capable of gaining. Before we rush to criticize them, however, we might do well to reflect that our performance may often be no better.

For discussion:

1. In what way was it appropriate for Jesus to quote from Isaiah chapter 6?
2. In what sense do Jesus' words either change us or judge us?
3. Why is the lack of faith of the townspeople a prohibitive factor in Jesus' ability to do any miracles in Nazareth? What would have been the likely outcome if he had done miracles?
4. Do you think that if we have a small view of God it can affect what he is able to do a) in our lives and b) in our church?
5. These disciples had earlier entrusted their entire lives to following Jesus, but struggled with times like this. Is this the paralyzing effect of fear in a crisis, or something else?
6. What makes it difficult for us to trust in the Lord in challenging situations?

CHAPTER FIVE: THE HEART OF THE PROBLEM: SYMPTOMS, DIAGNOSIS AND CURE

In some parts of the world there are some strange traditions. For example, do you know about the biggest tomato fight in the world? La Tomatina, the annual Tomato Throwing Festival, is held in the Valencian town of Buñol, Spain. It's held on the last Wednesday of August, and the participants throw tomatoes and get involved purely for fun.

There are many theories about Tomatina. In 1945, during a parade (of gigantes y cabezudos), young adults who wanted to be involved in it staged a brawl in the town's main square, the Plaza del Pueblo. There was a vegetable stand nearby, so they picked up tomatoes and used them as weapons. The police had to intervene to break up the fight and forced those responsible to pay the damages incurred. This is the most popular of many theories about how the Tomatina started.

The Jews of Jesus' time had their own traditional practices. These tended to be excessive add-on practices built on to the Old Testament law, and they were a source of some debate between the religious leaders and Jesus. The 'elders' made up rules or 'traditions' thinking they were helping the Jews to keep God's law better. But it's always dangerous to add to God's laws. Our rules and traditions can become more important to us than God's own actual laws (Mark 7:8). At times, it led the Jewish religious leaders to neglect and invalidate God's original intention, as they effectively got things back to front or inside out.

These Jews wanted to look good on the outside. But that's not God's focus at all. God requires us to be good on the inside. What's challenging is we're not immune to thinking the same way as those religious leaders did. It might be good to ask ourselves: 'What things do we do to make ourselves look good on the outside? Maybe that's why we go to church … or say prayers … and give to charity?

At the beginning of chapter 7 of Mark's Gospel, we encounter the religious leaders of Israel picking a fight over the issue of Jesus' disciples not washing their hands often enough:

> *"The Pharisees and some of the scribes gathered around Him when they had come from Jerusalem, and had seen that some of His disciples were eating their bread with impure hands, that is, unwashed. (For the Pharisees and all the Jews do not eat unless they carefully wash their hands, thus observing the traditions of the elders; and when they come from the market place, they do not eat unless they cleanse themselves; and there are many other things which they have received in order to observe, such as the washing of cups and pitchers and copper pots.*
>
> *The Pharisees and the scribes asked Him, "Why do Your disciples not walk according to the tradition of the elders, but eat their bread with impure hands?"*

And He said to them, "Rightly did Isaiah prophesy of you hypocrites, as it is written: 'THIS PEOPLE HONORS ME WITH THEIR LIPS, BUT THEIR HEART IS FAR AWAY FROM ME. 'BUT IN VAIN DO THEY WORSHIP ME, TEACHING AS DOCTRINES THE PRECEPTS OF MEN.' Neglecting the commandment of God, you hold to the tradition of men." He was also saying to them, "You are experts at setting aside the commandment of God in order to keep your tradition" (Mark 7:1-9).

Jesus identifies the underlying issue for them. They were much more focused on their own additional rules than on God's original laws. Jesus then gave a pin-sharp analysis of their religious performance by homing in on one telling example:

"For Moses said, 'HONOR YOUR FATHER AND YOUR MOTHER'; and, 'HE WHO SPEAKS EVIL OF FATHER OR MOTHER, IS TO BE PUT TO DEATH'; but you say, 'If a man says to his father or his mother, whatever I have that would help you is Corban (that is to say, given to God),' you no longer permit him to do anything for his father or his mother; thus invalidating the word of God by your tradition which you have handed down; and you do many things such as that" (Mark 7:10-13).

The example Jesus chose, showed the truth about these Jews. How they kept their own rules ('Corban') because it made them look good. They didn't keep God's law ('honour your parents') because they didn't love God. They loved their religion, not God!

They kept their rules on the outside, but didn't obey God's commands in their hearts. Going back to the original issue about hand-washing, Jesus shows them the basic error in their thinking. Behind all wrong behaviour there's always wrong thinking. It's important to be clear that this discussion isn't at all to do with hygiene, but is about ceremonial ritual with its symbolic meaning. They were worried sin would enter into them from outside, but it's already inside (and liable to spread)! Food from outside can't make us 'unclean' in God's eyes. Sin coming out from within our hearts is what makes us dirty. The heart is where the problem originates - from deep inside us, where only God can change us. Jesus was saying that the heart of the human problem is the problem of the human heart.

In some places, people ask you to take your shoes off when you come from outside. However, inside their homes are already many 'dirty' things. Bad words, bad feelings, bad programs on television. The real dirt is inside the home. Many people think that they must be good externally. They try to do good things through their religion. Just like the Pharisees – no better, no different. What they really need is a new heart! Religion sets rules; Jesus sets free. Religion is man-made. The Pharisees thought sin came from outside of ourselves. They washed in a religious way so that they didn't eat anything 'unclean.' But Jesus says food goes into the stomach and out the other end! This has nothing to do with sin! The real dirt is inside already.

Aleksandr Solzhenitsyn once said: 'If only there were evil people somewhere insidiously committing evil deeds, and it were necessary only to separate them from the rest of us and destroy them. But the line dividing good and evil cuts through the heart of every human being.' I don't know to what extent he was aware of it, but he was endorsing the diagnosis of the human problem that Jesus Christ gave here in Mark chapter 7:

> *"For from within, out of the heart of men, proceed the evil thoughts, fornications, thefts, murders, adulteries, deeds of coveting and wickedness, as well as deceit, sensuality, envy, slander, pride and foolishness. All these things proceed from within and defile the man"* (Mark 7:20-23).

Notice how we move from symptoms to diagnosis to cure, as we read about the Divine Physician, Jesus Christ, whom Mark from the beginning of his book has declared to be the son of God.

The diagnosis is: *"The heart is more deceitful than all else and is desperately sick"* (Jeremiah 17:9). As we say, the heart of the problem is the problem of the heart. Much earlier in human history, Moses wrote: *"the LORD saw that ... every intent of the thoughts of his heart was only evil continually"* (Genesis 6:5). The Lord Jesus is affirming here that nothing has changed.

Later, his Apostles would spread his message of the only effective remedy for sin. We read of the cure in the book of Acts: about *"Cleansing ... hearts by faith"* (Acts 15:9). It's got nothing to do with our religious works; it's believing fully in God's work. By faith we receive from God a new heart (this is what it means to be 'born again' as a new person – to use the words Jesus himself coined as he spoke with one of the Jewish religious leaders in John chapter 3).

God had promised this same remedy was coming long before. We remember how Mark introduced Jesus as someone promised back in Old Testament times (Mark 1:15). The prophet Ezekiel, writing in the Bible, had predicted a time of which God had said to his ancient people:

> *"I will cleanse you from all your filthiness ... I will give you a new heart and put a new spirit within you; and I will remove the heart of stone from your flesh and give you a heart of flesh. I will put My Spirit within you and cause you to walk in My statutes, and you will be careful to observe My ordinances"* (Ezekiel 36:25-27).

This does seem to be what lies behind Jesus' description of *"being born of water and of the Spirit"* in John 3:5.

In stark contrast to this is the big religious lie that says if we do our best when we stand before God one day, he'll look at the good things we've done and also the bad things we've done, and if the good outweighs the bad, he'll let us into heaven. That's pretty much a summing up of any man-made religion. It is not God's message of salvation from sin which is preached in the Bible, including by Jesus Christ. Our problem in God's sight is internal, reaching to the core of our being. We need a new heart, a new birth. This is what faith in Christ brings about. It's the miracle God performs for every true believer in his son.

For discussion:

1. What things do we do to make ourselves look good on the outside?
2. Give some examples of (any) religion showing its preoccupation with externals.
3. We've characterized 'the big religious lie' as the idea that if we do our best, then when we stand before God one day, he'll look at the good things we've done and also the bad things we've done, and if the good outweighs the bad, he'll let us into heaven. What things does the religion you're most familiar with regard as 'good things to do'?
4. In the words of Jesus, pinpoint the symptoms, diagnosis and cure of the human condition.

CHAPTER SIX: THE CHANGING OF AN ERA / MOVING INTO GENTILE TERRITORY

No doubt you've seen those pairs of pictures found in puzzle books for children, mainly. They're almost identical, but there are very subtle differences, and the name of the game is to find those tiny differences. It's an exercise in keen observation. Bearing that in mind, I want to pose a 'spot the difference' kind of question. What's the difference between the large-scale feeding Mark describes for us in chapter 6 of his Gospel; and the one he later describes in chapter 8. Yes, you'll tell me one featured five thousand men, and the other 4,000 persons. In the former we read of five loaves; while it was seven in the later and so on ... including the different number of baskets of fragments gathered up at the end.

But that actually misses the point. Mark has written the shortest Gospel of all. He doesn't detail the long speeches Jesus made. His writing is full of action. He keeps the pace up, frequently using the term 'immediately' - or 'straightway' in the older versions. Mark's writing style is very much to the point. There was an abundance of material to draw on from the life of the Lord Jesus, as one of the other Gospel writers, John, tells us. Mark was, therefore, being highly selective. And yet he includes two, on the face of it, very similar miracles performed by Jesus. Would it not seem to us to be the obvious economy to make: to let one recorded large-scale feeding miracle suffice to make the point that Jesus could do this kind of thing?

To sum up: why include two stories about large numbers being fed? (Mark 6:30-44 and Mark 8:1-10). This is obviously deliberate, it's clearly by design. It's making a point – but what point? As always, the context gives us a vital clue, and opens up some really important teaching.

The first thing to notice is that Jesus is now journeying through Gentile areas. He goes to Tyre (Mark 7:24), and then on to Decapolis (Mark 7:31). Later, we read that Jesus went back to Dalmanutha (Mark 8:10) back on the Jewish side of the lake again. Just before that return to the Jewish area, Mark in his write-up of the feeding of the 4,000 uses a different word for 'basket' (Mark 8:8); different from the earlier mention of 'basket' in relation to the feeding of the 5,000 (Mark 6:43). Could it be because Gentiles used a different kind of basket from Jews?

In the last paragraph of chapter 7 and in the first paragraph of chapter 8, Mark sketches three incidents in Gentile territory. We begin our review with the exorcism found in Mark 7:24 until the end of the chapter. Is this just yet another exorcism? No, we get, in fact, 3 mentions of 'Gentile-ness' (in vv.24,26) in connection with it. First, we're informed Jesus had come 'to the region of Tyre.' It was while he was there that a woman came to meet him. Mark says, *'the woman was a Gentile'* ... *'of the Syrophoenician race.'* This repetition, surely for emphasis, sends the hidden message: this was someone who wasn't entitled to anything from God, but by grace could be included.

It can hardly be doubted that the subtext here is that 'Jesus is willing to accept anyone who wants to trust him.' It doesn't matter who you are; no matter how bad, or even simply if you don't come from a Christian family. We can all be like this woman and bring our need to Jesus, begging him to help us. Later in the Bible, the Apostle Paul will remind Gentile Christians: *"you were ... separate ... excluded ... strangers ... having no hope and without God in the world"* (Ephesians 2:12).

Mark's making an important point here. For the Jews thought the Gentiles weren't clean ... that God had no interest in them. I wonder, do we look down on some people? (Remember how Jonah did – and God had to teach him a lesson). It's true Jesus didn't go looking for Gentile people, as that was not his mission. God's salvation was to the Jew first, and Jesus was sent to the lost sheep of Israel. I've just mentioned sheep there in relation to the Jews, but the Jews sometimes called the Gentiles 'dogs.' Sounds unkind, doesn't it, but Jesus is never rude, and he takes up that terminology here in conversation with this begging Gentile woman who wants Jesus to exorcize the demon or unclean spirit from her daughter.

Is it possible that the Lord was testing her? In effect, saying: 'You know what the Jews think of you. So why have you come to me?' If so, Jesus only wants to bring her faith out into the open.

As Mark records this meeting between Jesus and the Gentile mother, it may strike us as an awkward exchange. It goes like this: 'please, heal my daughter' ... 'why should I give you food?' Then there's talk of mere crumbs! She's not offended – she was more than happy with scraps, it would seem. Jesus is impressed! This is foreign to our 21st-century western sense of entitlement, isn't it? We get inclusiveness drummed into us, along with the idea that everyone has rights - even equal rights. Mark wants us to register the point here: God doesn't owe us anything! Shame on us if we thought God owed us anything.

The woman is desperate. She doesn't even wait for Jesus to come out of the house! She enters it. Jesus had wanted to be alone with his disciples, but still, he didn't tell her to go away. Jesus always has time for people who need him. For her part, the woman is humble. She doesn't mind when Jesus refers to dogs – and to her by association. She doesn't shoot back: 'I'm as good as any Jew!' She knows she doesn't deserve anything from Jesus. Rather, she 'begs' Jesus. She doesn't say: 'Perhaps you can help me.' She knows Jesus can drive out the demon and keeps on asking. When Jesus tests her faith, she doesn't give up. She doesn't mind being a 'dog', if she can have the crumbs from the table! She accepts what Jesus says (Mark 7:29). She's happy to go home, because she trusts Jesus and expects to find her daughter well. Remember the disciples are watching Jesus – they've not often seen Jews believe like this! But this Gentile woman really believes!

Well, the second incident that Mark records for us as having taken place in Gentile territory is a miraculous feeding. With the woman, as we've just heard, there was talk of crumbs. Now there's mention of much more than crumbs! In fact, it's a banquet! How often we ask God for crumbs and we receive a banquet. Across the three chapters (Mark 6,7 & 8), we read: *"all ate and were satisfied"* (Mark 6:42), *"... let the children be satisfied"*

(Mark 7:27), and *"... they ate and were satisfied"* (Mark 8:8). Only God can satisfy. Remember, John in his Gospel, when presenting the feeding of the 5,000, presents it as a sign that Jesus alone can satisfy the spiritual hunger of each and every human heart.

Let's be clear: God's Old Testament purposes were not ethnically all-inclusive. Israel was the favoured nation back then. But at this point in his Gospel, Mark is indicating that a change is coming – it's a momentous change. The first indication of this breaking news was in Mark 7:19 when the comment was added that Jesus had declared all foods clean. It would no longer be a restricted 'kosher' menu. The same message was reinforced to the Apostle Peter to prepare him for his first preaching contact with Gentiles. What happened with Peter at Caesarea in Acts 10 has often being termed 'a Gentile Pentecost' after the Jewish Pentecost when the Holy Spirit descended in Acts chapter 2. Anyway, coming back to Mark's Gospel – this is a vital section, because otherwise nothing previous would apply to any of us reading the text as Gentiles. This is the breaking news that the introduction of the king, the announcement of the kingdom, and the demonstration of its authority are all, in fact, very relevant to us Gentiles – as well as to Jews!

Jesus shows the same love for these Gentile people as for his own people. He cares just as much that they're hungry. He feeds 4,000 Gentiles in the same way as he fed 5,000 Jewish people in Mark 6. Imagine what the disciples thought of this! Remember they didn't respect Gentiles. They thought God only cared about Jews – that he was exclusively pro-Semitic.

After the feeding of the 4,000, the third miracle in this sequence features a deaf man. He's probably also a Gentile, based on the context. This was a miracle with a message. The disciples were deaf in another way. We, too, need Jesus to open our ears so we can believe (and we need Jesus to open our mouths so that we can tell people about him). Why does Jesus make this miracle seem harder? Is it because Jesus sees people and even his own disciples as being like this man – they're deaf to God's truth? Whenever he asks them not to tell others about him it's because Jesus didn't want them to give the wrong message about him – he's not just 'the man who does miracles'! Not even his disciples know the full story yet.

The man at the centre of this third Gentile miracle can't hear, so Jesus uses sign language; he does things that he can see. He puts his fingers in the man's ear and touches his tongue. This would clearly show his intention to heal. Next Jesus looks up to heaven – possibly communicating to the man that he needs God's miracle. In fact, we all need God's miracle: it's not enough to hear about Jesus - we need Jesus to open our ears so we can understand (and, later, we need Jesus to open our mouths so we can tell people who he is).

A final thought about the feeding of the 4,000. Many people liked the miracle, but they didn't see who Jesus was. They didn't think: 'If Jesus makes bread and fish for us, he must be God.' They didn't follow Jesus, they just went home. Is that not a bit like those today who applaud the good fortune that all the conditions for life were coincidentally met on this tiny planet. That this 'just right' quality of our planet was a freak cosmic accident is taken for granted. A shrug of the shoulders and they get on with life.

TAKE YOUR MARK'S GOSPEL

For discussion:

1. In your own words, why did Mark include 2 stories about large numbers being fed (Mark 6:30-44 & Mark 8:1-10)?
2. How did the first miracle in Gentile territory make this same point about inclusiveness in the Gospel Age?
3. Sometimes God's ways are hard to understand. Jesus' treatment of the Gentile woman might initially seem to be like that. In the light of the outcome, how might we view it?
4. Why, do you think, Jesus gives a sigh when healing the deaf man?

CHAPTER SEVEN: GAINING INSIGHT AT LAST

In this section of Mark's Gospel, we're reminded: first, of how Herod would not repent; second, that the Pharisees were unable or unwilling to believe (no matter how many signs they saw); and third, how a seemingly trivial conversation about lunch showed the same faithless tendency characterizing Jesus' own disciples.

It all follows on from the miraculous feeding of the 4,000. It was directly after Jesus' return to the Jewish region again, that ...

> *"The Pharisees came out and began to argue with Him, seeking from Him a sign from heaven, to test Him. Sighing deeply in His spirit, He said, "Why does this generation seek for a sign? Truly I say to you, no sign will be given to this generation." Leaving them, He again embarked and went away to the other side. And they had forgotten to take bread, and did not have more than one loaf in the boat with them. And He was giving orders to them, saying, "Watch out! Beware of the leaven of the Pharisees and the leaven of Herod." They began to discuss with one another the fact that they had no bread"* (Mark 8:11-16).

I just want to interrupt the reading there to prepare for the fact that Jesus is now going to begin to fire off 8 questions in the 5 verses that follow. Listen out for them. Eight questions in quick succession shows significant emotional investment by the Lord in this issue surrounding the disciples' lack of faith. That alone makes it worthy of our keenest attention. We need to ask 'just what is going on here?' Now for those questions ...

> *And Jesus, aware of this, said to them, "Why do you discuss the fact that you have no bread? Do you not yet see or understand? Do you have a hardened heart? "HAVING EYES, DO YOU NOT SEE? AND HAVING EARS, DO YOU NOT HEAR? And do you not remember, when I broke the five loaves for the five thousand, how many baskets full of broken pieces you picked up?" They said to Him, "Twelve." "When I broke the seven for the four thousand, how many large baskets full of broken pieces did you pick up?" And they said to Him, "Seven." And He was saying to them, "Do you not yet understand?"* (Mark 8:17-21).

Ok, let's begin by asking 'What's Jesus saying about leaven or yeast?' For, it was when the disciples were discussing Jesus' mention of leaven that the Lord began the series of questions. Let's rewind to verse 15 again: *"And He was giving orders to them, saying, "Watch out! Beware of the leaven of the Pharisees and the leaven of Herod."*

What does Jesus mean? What does the leaven represent? The leaven of the Pharisees can't refer to their teaching, as that meaning would make no sense when we come to relate it to Herod - for Jesus equally spoke of the leaven of Herod. What we have already encountered in Mark's Gospel is the fact that Herod would not repent; and the Pharisees have been shown to be unable or unwilling to believe in Jesus (no matter how many signs). The overall correct response to the message Jesus brings is to repent and believe – to repent and believe that Jesus has come to rescue his people in a greater way than Moses.

The disciples were concerned about how to feed themselves with only one loaf of bread. Jesus takes them back to the feeding of the 5,000, and then on to the feeding of the 4,000. They recollect and affirm the facts. It's not a memory lapse or intellectual difficulty that they're having. But it's as if they've not processed this information. They've not drawn the obvious conclusion about the new Moses, the new deliverer - the person they're following. This begins to amount, on their part, to rebellious ignorance! Jesus' reference in the imagery of the yeast is a reference to the leaven of culpable, wilful ignorance. Their hearts were hard, they were lacking insight – in other words, just like Herod and the Pharisees (Mark 3:1-6)!

Jesus then uses a phrase coined by Jeremiah (in Jeremiah 5:19-21) and Ezekiel (in Ezekiel 12:1-2) about eyes that don't see and ears that can't hear. These quotes show God's judgement on morally culpable people is to blind and deafen them. They'd seen Jesus do so much, they'd heard Jesus say so much. But the disciples are still blind. They cannot see who Jesus is. Their hearts are still hard and they don't believe. Just like the Pharisees! (Mark 3:5; Mark 6:52; Mark 7:17-18). Like the disciples, our hearts are hard and we also need a miracle so that we believe in Jesus. Jesus warns his disciples not to be like the Pharisees and Herod. People use yeast in baking bread, to make it rise as it spreads through the bread mixture. 'Be careful!' he's saying, 'that the 'yeast' of the Pharisees doesn't spread to you, giving you the same hard hearts.'

But, wait a moment, let's apply this to ourselves, as well. We can become like the people close to us! (People who behave in the way Herod or the Pharisees behaved). Jesus says: 'Be careful of that yeast!' It can easily spread to us. We can be very slow to believe in Jesus.

Often, the miracles that the Lord Jesus performed had a teaching purpose, as well as bringing blessing to the person concerned. Mark now follows up the lesson about leaven with a description of a miracle done to a blind man. In a way, the disciples are all like spiritually blind men. They see the signs Jesus does, but due to having hard hearts they, too, refuse to believe Jesus' true identity. In a very real sense, the disciples need a miracle! And the next thing we read about is, in fact, a miracle! It's one in which a blind man sees. It's another miracle with a message (like Mark 7:31-35). The healing of the blind man points to the solution.

> *"And they came to Bethsaida. And they brought a blind man to Jesus and implored Him to touch him. Taking the blind man by the hand, He brought him out of the village; and after spitting on his eyes and laying His hands on him, He asked him, "Do you see anything?" And he looked up and said, "I see men, for I see them like trees, walking around." Then again He laid His hands on his eyes; and he looked intently and was restored, and began to see everything clearly. And*

He sent him to his home, saying, "Do not even enter the village" (Mark 8:22-26).

This is a miracle with a difference. Jesus touches the man's eyes twice - not because it didn't work well the first time. Jesus meant to do the miracle in two parts, because the miracle has a message. This man is like the disciples. Very soon, they'll see – but still only half see! Peter's eyes get opened - halfway, at least. Peter, like the man on whom the miracle was performed, can now see who Jesus is, but he's still half-blind. He doesn't yet understand why Jesus has come.

"Jesus went out, along with His disciples, to the villages of Caesarea Philippi; and on the way He questioned His disciples, saying to them, "Who do people say that I am?" They told Him, saying, "John the Baptist; and others say Elijah; but others, one of the prophets." And He continued by questioning them, "But who do you say that I am?" Peter answered and said to Him, "You are the Christ." And He warned them to tell no one about Him" (Mark 8:27-29).

Peter sees that Jesus is the Christ, but he doesn't see that Jesus must die (Mark 8:31, 32). Peter is like the man in Mark 8:24 – first blind, then only half-blind. For the rest of Mark's Gospel, the disciples are still half-blind. Jesus teaches them, but they don't see very well – in fact, they don't completely understand until Jesus rises from the dead.

We've talked about Mark's Gospel being a book of two halves – divided by this confession made by Peter, which is the middle

TAKE YOUR MARK'S GOSPEL

one of three confessions about Jesus being the Son of God. The first half of Mark's Gospel, up until this point, is focused on showing who Jesus is (chapters 1-8); afterwards, the concentration is on showing why he came (chapters 9-16).

Think about the actual blind man again for a moment. Jesus takes the man out of the village and doesn't want him to go back after. Jesus wants to keep this miracle quiet. It's been something for the disciples to think about. They mustn't tell people yet (Mark 8:30), because (like them) people have the wrong idea about 'the Christ' - they first need to see what Christ came to do.

'I can see!' Those are the best words a blind man can ever say! And 'You are the Christ!' are the best words Peter ever said! Other people say different things about Jesus, but Peter knows the truth and isn't afraid to say it. Perhaps like Peter you only half-see. There are still many things you don't understand. Don't be afraid to tell others that you believe in Jesus the Saviour. And, as you follow Jesus, he will help you to see more and more, and then you can share that also.

For discussion:

1. What characteristic of yeast / leaven was Jesus thinking of (v.15), and what did the leaven represent here?
2. What lesson did Jesus expect his disciples to learn from the various feedings (v.21)?
3. Why did the Lord heal the blind man in two stages?
4. What was the significance of Peter's confession (v.29)?
5. Why did Jesus ask his disciples not to repeat this revelation to others?
6. In what ways might we be guilty of hardness of heart (see Hebrew 3:4) as we are influenced by society around us?

CHAPTER EIGHT: SEEING HALF THE PICTURE

We've arrived at the halfway point of Mark's version of the story of Jesus' life on earth. His Gospel hinges on the confession Peter made when in answer to Jesus' question: 'Who do you say that I am?', Peter had answered: 'You are the Christ.' To any Jew, this was a reference to the one they were all expecting. The term 'Christ' literally means 'the Anointed.' Jesus, Peter confessed, was the promised anointed king. Mark has been arranging his narration of Jesus' life so as to provide us with evidence of Jesus' authority.

Mark has previously told us about a man whose blindness Jesus healed in two stages. At the halfway point of his miraculous healing, he could only half-see – in other words, in fact in his own words, he saw *"men as trees walking,"* which obviously means he saw things, but they weren't sharply in focus. At this halfway point of Mark's Gospel, Peter and the disciples are also at the half-blind stage. They've got half the picture. They now believe Jesus is the king, but they misunderstand why he has come. Of course, the assumption is that a king will ascend the throne and benefit his people. Like others belonging to his nation, Peter is expecting that Jesus will restore Israel's fortunes, and rid them of their Roman masters.

For all those, like Peter, who were thinking along those lines at that time, what Jesus said next was really shocking ...

> *"He began to teach them that the Son of Man must suffer many things and be rejected by the elders and the chief priests and the scribes, and be killed, and after three days rise again. And He was stating the matter plainly. And Peter took Him aside and began to rebuke Him. But turning around and seeing His disciples, He rebuked Peter and said, "Get behind Me, Satan; for you are not setting your mind on God's interests, but man's"* (Mark 8:31-33).

Upon Peter's confession, Jesus warned the disciples to tell no-one about him. The reason for this would become clear immediately. It was because they as yet only had half the story. Jesus went on to tell them that he hadn't come to be made king. To encourage the inappropriate ambitions of others would be a problem.

Rather, Jesus tells them that he'd come to die. He did this to correct their natural, but mistaken view, of the anointed king. This was not the time for him to restore the kingdom to Israel. The culmination of his present mission on earth would not be a crown and a throne, but in fact it was going to be a cross and a tomb. It's hard for us to realize just how nonsensical this would have seemed to Peter and the other disciples. Christ and crucify were oxymoronic – in other words, Christ and crucify were words that couldn't be connected in a single sentence nor indeed have anything in common.

But here was Jesus plainly saying that the Son of Man – by which he referred to himself – was going to suffer. The Jews had never seen this coming. They read and loved the writings of the Bible prophets, but somehow they'd all been blinded to this. It's true that Bible prophets, such as Daniel, had shared visions of a glorious reigning 'son of man.' But, on the other hand, Bible prophets, such as Isaiah, had written of God's servant who would suffer. We all have a tendency to hear only what we want to hear, and to filter out what doesn't appeal or doesn't even make sense to us. Whenever – to this day – when Jews read the Old Testament, they do this. But, the text is clear when it describes both the glories and the sufferings of its central figure, the one the Jewish people were waiting for. Jesus, and later his disciples, would clarify that the sufferings came first, then the glories. It was through sufferings that the long-expected king would enter into his glories.

In fact, it must be this way. Jesus plainly now declares that he, the son of man, must suffer. That was too much for Peter. He at once protested that this could never be. With his characteristic forwardness, Peter actually took Jesus to one side and rebuked him for saying such an impossible thing. The Lord, who moments before had told Peter that he'd been blessed with God-given insight into Jesus' true identity, sharply rebuked Peter. Jesus recognized that the Devil was using Peter as his spokesperson at that moment, in what would be another futile attempt to divert him from his path to the cross. Jesus told Peter that he was guilty of being focused on human interests, and not on God's interests.

God's plan in sending his son, Jesus, into this world, was centred on the cross. Peter would not be the last follower of Jesus who wrongly thought that following Jesus is the way to prosperity now.

Many of us have probably seen the famous advertisement which, as the story goes, Ernest Shackleton ran in the newspaper to try to recruit men for his *Endurance* expedition:

Men wanted for hazardous journey. Low wages, bitter cold, long hours of complete darkness. Safe return doubtful. Honour and recognition in event of success.

This advertisement is one of the most famous in history. It's frequently quoted as one of the best examples of copy writing, and has been quoted many times. However, its origins are obscure. No one has actually seen the ad printed in a newspaper, though the Antarctic Circle has a $100 reward out for anyone who can find it, a reward which has not yet been claimed. Be that as it may, the popularity of this advert – apocryphal or otherwise – encourages me to quote it once again, but only to highlight the much more far-reaching 'advert' for Christian discipleship that Jesus himself has 'posted.' Compare this ...

> *"And He summoned the crowd with His disciples, and said to them, "If anyone wishes to come after Me, he must deny himself, and take up his cross and follow Me. For whoever wishes to save his life will lose it, but whoever loses his life for My sake and the gospel's will save it. For what does it profit a man to gain the whole world, and forfeit his soul? For what will a man give in exchange for his soul? For whoever is ashamed of Me and My words in this adulterous and sinful generation, the Son of Man will also be ashamed of him when He comes in the glory of His Father with the holy angels"* (Mark 8:34-38).

As with the king, so with his subjects: the way to glory is through suffering. Christians, if authentic followers of Christ, were never promised an easy life. It's quite rational, if in this world only, we should wish to save our life. However, when we bring faith into the frame, and extend our thoughts to consider also the world to come, then it becomes perfectly rational to choose to lose our life in this world. The reason being that's the way to save it in the world to come - which is a more meaningful thing to do. For most of Christ's followers, this will not be about martyrdom – as it would turn out to be for those earliest followers – but about self-sacrificing choices now based on faith in a longer-term investment beyond this life. In the next chapter, the Lord explains that those who are divorced must deny themselves the right to another marriage. For others, it may be embracing the shame of aligning with the Bible's plain teaching. Jesus then continued to address his disciples ...

> *"Truly I say to you, there are some of those who are standing here who will not taste death until they see the kingdom of God after it has come with power." Six days later, Jesus took with Him Peter and James and John, and brought them up on a high mountain by themselves. And He was transfigured before them; and His garments became radiant and exceedingly white, as no launderer on earth can whiten them. Elijah appeared to them along with Moses; and they were talking with Jesus. Peter said to Jesus, "Rabbi, it is good for us to be here; let us make three tabernacles, one for You, and one for Moses, and one for Elijah." For he did not know what to answer; for they became terrified.*

Then a cloud formed, overshadowing them, and a voice came out of the cloud, "This is My beloved Son, listen to Him!" All at once they looked around and saw no one with them anymore, except Jesus alone. As they were coming down from the mountain, He gave them orders not to relate to anyone what they had seen, until the Son of Man rose from the dead. They seized upon that statement, discussing with one another what rising from the dead meant. They asked Him, saying, "Why is it that the scribes say that Elijah must come first?" And He said to them, "Elijah does first come and restore all things. And yet how is it written of the Son of Man that He will suffer many things and be treated with contempt? But I say to you that Elijah has indeed come, and they did to him whatever they wished, just as it is written of him" (Mark 9:1-13).

In coming to earth as a man, Jesus, God's son, had emptied himself of all visible splendour like this. To stimulate the faith of Peter, James and John, they were given this glimpse. Moses, one of the two Old Testament characters to appear with him, had once asked: *"Show me Your glory."* Surely, this episode was a bonus: to be seen with the Lord in his glory in the Promised (Holy) Land! But then Peter's ill-considered comment got him into further trouble. He offered to make three booths, one each for Jesus, Moses and Elijah. The reprimand, this time, came from heaven. It singled out Jesus as the one to listen to. This makes the point that we shouldn't put anyone on a par with Jesus. Sadly, that's what this world's religions do. Mark, here, makes it very plain: Jesus Christ, the son of God, is incomparable. What this episode also emphasizes again is the way to glory is through suffering. The other Gospel writers tell us that the topic of Moses and Elijah's conversation with Jesus was all about his death or exit from this world. The glorious backdrop for this solemn topic demonstrated graphically that Jesus would ascend from the shameful cross to the glorious throne in heaven. After his present sufferings, there would indeed be future and eternal glory.

For discussion:

1. In what way was Peter still half-blind?
2. Jesus delights to call himself by the title of 'Son of Man' taken from Daniel's description of someone he saw in a vision (Daniel 7:13). How would this background have fuelled Peter's misunderstanding?
3. Jesus' listeners did not know the kind of death he would die, so what do you think they would have understood by 'taking up their cross' (Mark 8:34)
4. Is it only an unbeliever who can 'save his life' (v.35)?
5. Why, do you think, Peter, James and John were favoured with these experiences above the others of the Twelve?

CHAPTER NINE: LOSING LIFE, DENYING SELF AND BECOMING LITTLE

Mark has just described the mountain-top scene when Jesus underwent a change that briefly allowed Peter and two other disciples to see his glory. We're left wondering why this happened. Why does Mark write about that here? There must be a connection with what has just gone before. And what was that? It was the first plain mention to his disciples of what lay ahead for Jesus at Jerusalem: in other words, his crucifixion. Coming immediately on the heels of the confirmation that he was the Christ, the long-awaited king, this seemed a total contradiction to these disciples. What's more, Jesus had gone on to speak of how, in following him, the disciples could expect to lose their lives. Two of those who saw Jesus' glory were James and John, who were still dreaming of being next to Jesus when he would shortly set up his kingdom on earth (Mark 10:32-45, assuming the James mentioned to be John's brother). They'd still to realize that before future glory with Jesus, there lay a path of shame and self-denial. Beyond that, could it be that the mountain scene was intended as a reassurance that the future glory was for real?

But then we come down to earth with a bang. For, descending to the foot of the mountain, they rejoin the rest of the disciples who've been struggling and failing to effect an exorcism. It's a pathetic case. In fact, Mark gives us here one of the longest and most graphic accounts of any victim: a young boy, writhing on the ground. Perhaps, as a doctor would, Jesus asks the boy's father how long it's been like this. Lifelong, is the reply, 'from childhood.' That enquiry tests the father's faith, for he pleads: *'... if You can do anything ...!'* *'If You can?'* Jesus repeats, before saying, *'All things are possible to him who believes.'* At once the father confesses this lapse and asks the Lord to help his unbelief. At this, Jesus commanded the evil spirit to leave the boy, which it does, but not before appearing to leave the boy looking 'so much like a corpse' that many there declared that he was in fact dead. But Jesus raised him up, and all was well. The language here reminds us that Jesus has been teaching a lot recently about death and resurrection and about his followers losing life now and saving it in the next world. This takes faith, and that's the lesson highlighted from this incident too.

It seems as if Mark is presenting things in threes at the moment, for we now come to the second of three occasions in three successive chapters when Jesus plainly tells his followers that he's heading towards a shameful death before being raised from the dead in glory.

In talking about this, Jesus consistently uses an Old Testament title for himself as Son of Man. Back in the Old Testament, prophets such as Daniel had associated it with their expected king who'd come to reign in glory. Now Jesus is repeatedly using it in connection with terrible suffering. This is really hard for these disciples to get their heads around. They're confused, and it just doesn't register. The fact they can't compute it might excuse in part their really inappropriate response whenever Jesus talks like this. Each time, in Mark's Gospel chapters 8, 9 and 10 when Jesus shares the sad news of the painful death that awaits him, the disciples – on each and every occasion – think of their own interests (Mark 8:33), about which of them is the greatest (Mark 9:34), and who will get the best seats in the house (Mark 10:35-37). This is crass insensitivity in the extreme, but it happens every time! Jesus is focused on losing his life, but his disciples are seemingly obsessed with saving theirs.

Displaying the most remarkable patience, Jesus sat down with them and explained that the way to being first was to become last and least (Mark 9:35). Jesus drove home the point with an object lesson. He set a young child before these power-hungry men, and then, embracing the child, explained that to receive a child in Jesus' name was to receive Jesus himself. It was easy to dismiss children in those days as insignificant – and Mark over the page (Mark 10:13) records an example of these very disciples shooing away children in case they should bother Jesus. Jesus stopped them doing that and reinforced the same lesson, again taking the children in his arms. What is it with children?

Well, children are generally oblivious to others' reputation and blind to differences of class and status. Like their master, Jesus, the disciples would need to be ready to make themselves of no reputation and accept the need to become little before they could ever be big. Jesus also went on to warn his followers in the strongest terms that they should be careful so as not to mislead any 'little ones who believe' (Mark 9:42). What an amazing teacher Jesus is, and how expertly he put his points across!

At this point, at the opening of chapter 10 of his Gospel, Mark chooses to insert a record of a testy conversation the religious leaders, or Pharisees, initiated with Jesus. It was on the vexed topic of what are legitimate grounds for divorce. These religious leaders were being quite insincere: their only interest in Jesus' answer was to create controversy by attempting to have Jesus identify himself with one or other side in an on-going heated debate of those times. How hard or easy would Jesus make divorce? But with perfect wisdom, Jesus neatly avoided the trap by returning them to God's original standard for marriage right from the beginning of the book of Genesis. Back then, Jesus was saying, in God's plan divorce was never in the frame at all.

There's no doubt the strength of Jesus' reply even took his own disciples by surprise, and they had to ask him privately for further confirmation (Mark 10:10). It was as if Jesus – in the wider context of this section of Mark's Gospel – was saying, 'Do you remember I was telling you about losing your life in this world for my sake? Well, here's an example of the sort of self-denial that following me involves. It may mean for you that you must surrender the right to another marriage that others enjoy after they've divorced.' After this, Mark narrates an interesting incident:

> *"As He was setting out on a journey, a man ran up to Him and knelt before Him, and asked Him, "Good Teacher, what shall I do to inherit eternal life?" And Jesus said to him, "Why do you call Me good? No one is good except God alone. "You know the commandments, 'DO NOT MURDER, DO NOT COMMIT ADULTERY, DO NOT STEAL, DO NOT BEAR FALSE WITNESS, Do not defraud, HONOR YOUR FATHER AND MOTHER.'" And he said to*

> *Him, "Teacher, I have kept all these things from my youth up." Looking at him, Jesus felt a love for him and said to him, "One thing you lack: go and sell all you possess and give to the poor, and you will have treasure in heaven; and come, follow Me." But at these words he was saddened, and he went away grieving, for he was one who owned much property.*
>
> *And Jesus, looking around, said to His disciples, "How hard it will be for those who are wealthy to enter the kingdom of God!" The disciples were amazed at His words. But Jesus answered again and said to them, "Children, how hard it is to enter the kingdom of God! "It is easier for a camel to go through the eye of a needle than for a rich man to enter the kingdom of God." They were even more astonished and said to Him, "Then who can be saved?" Looking at them, Jesus said, "With people it is impossible, but not with God; for all things are possible with God"* (Mark 10:17-27).

That's a faith-inspiring statement we should repeat and emphasize: what's impossible for us, is possible for God. You remember when Mark told us earlier in this section about when the disciples couldn't perform the exorcism of the boy whose case notes we were given in great detail? The lesson back then was: all things are possible to him who believes in God. That strengthened the faith of the boy's father; and encouraged faith expressed through prayer on the part of the disciples. Here, in dealing with the question posed: 'What must I do to inherit eternal life?' it's about faith for salvation – salvation meaning knowing all our sins are forgiven and we're no longer guilty before a holy God.

At the beginning of his answer to this questioner, Jesus picked up on his polite mode of address when he addressed Jesus as 'Good Teacher.' It's not enough to think of Jesus as only a good man, a good moral teacher. In God's sight, the Bible (in Romans 3:12) diagnoses none of us humans as being good. Jesus, however, was not denying that he was good, but rather affirming he was both good and God, for God alone is good – and we are not.

Next, Jesus mentioned five or six of the Ten Commandments, all focused on how we should lovingly treat our neighbours. Why does Jesus do this, we might wonder? The Bible is adamant that our own works cannot bring us salvation and eternal life. For example, Ephesians 2:8 says we are saved by God's grace through faith and not by our own works, for salvation is a gift God gives to those who believe. Why then does Jesus list several commands? There are at least two possibilities. His follow-up challenge to the young enquirer was about going away and giving all he possessed to help the poor. Perhaps this was to show that by failing to do this, the young man was wrong to claim he was loving his neighbour in an absolutely perfect way? Or, maybe, this man's money was his god – which was why Jesus hadn't yet dealt with those commands about loving God first in our lives.

In either case, and this is the main point, Jesus showed that even the best of us cannot humanly satisfy the demands of God's law in our own strength. It's impossible. The disciples at that time understood rich people to have been favoured by God, so if they could not be saved then what hope was there for others? Jesus confirmed that salvation is impossible for humans to achieve by themselves – no matter whatever amount of religious work is performed to try to impress God, even as this man had attempted. But, wonderfully, Jesus explained that God has made salvation possible for all who believe.

Jesus ends this section by once more summing up the main message of these chapters: *"But many who are first will be last, and the last, first"* (Mark 10:31).

For discussion:

1. Why do you think Peter and the others were allowed to see Christ's glory?

2. Was this the fulfilment of the kingdom of God coming with power – was it (Mark 9:1ff), or was that something later?

3. How does Mark emphasize the struggle the disciples are having to accept the disclosure of Jesus' impending death?

4. How does the conversation with the polite enquirer clarify for us that religion is not the answer?

5. In what area does our faith need to be inspired by the fact that what's impossible for us is possible with God?

CHAPTER TEN: SAVIOUR OR JUDGE?

Recently, I visited a couple of cities where the rich and famous are known to live. What stood out most for me was the number of homeless poor who were walking the streets begging and sleeping in battered tents near to the mansions of the rich. I thought of Jesus' story of the rich man and Lazarus, the beggar, and their different attitudes to God and so their different destinies. We get a similar sense of rich and poor together in the way Mark arranges his material as we move now into the final section of his Gospel.

He's told us about the rich young ruler who came to Jesus to enquire about how he might possess eternal life. He turned away from Jesus, and left sorrowful. Now we read ...

> *"Then they came to Jericho. And as He was leaving Jericho with His disciples and a large crowd, a blind beggar named Bartimaeus, the son of Timaeus, was sitting by the road. When he heard that it was Jesus the Nazarene, he began to cry out and say, "Jesus, Son of David, have mercy on me!" Many were sternly telling him to be quiet, but he kept crying out all the more, "Son of David, have mercy on me!" And Jesus stopped and said, "Call him here." So they called the blind man, saying to him, "Take courage, stand up! He is calling for you." Throwing aside his cloak, he jumped up and came to Jesus. And answering him, Jesus said, "What do you want Me to do for you?"*

And the blind man said to Him, "Rabboni, I want to regain my sight!" And Jesus said to him, "Go; your faith has made you well." Immediately he regained his sight and began following Him on the road" (Mark 10:46-52).

Unlike the rich ruler, this blind beggar, once healed, began immediately to follow Jesus as he left Jericho and headed into Jerusalem. We're now at the end of Mark chapter ten. After chapters 8 through 10, we enter the final stage of Mark's Gospel. Jesus has now arrived at his final destination – the city of Jerusalem. This is where all the remaining action takes place. Mark is going to walk us through it.

Let me ask you: Are you ever guilty of repeating yourself? There are times when we do so deliberately for it to have a planned effect. Mark does that now. Listen to this...

"As they approached Jerusalem, at Bethphage and Bethany, near the Mount of Olives, He sent two of His disciples, and said to them, "Go into the village opposite you, and immediately as you enter it, you will find a colt tied there, on which no one yet has ever sat; untie it and bring it here. "If anyone says to you, 'Why are you doing this?' you say, 'The Lord has need of it'; and immediately he will send it back here." They went away and found a colt tied at the door, outside in the street; and they untied it. Some of the bystanders were saying to them, "What are you doing, untying the colt?" They spoke to them just as Jesus had told them, and they gave them permission. They brought

the colt to Jesus and put their coats on it; and He sat on it. And many spread their coats in the road, and others spread leafy branches which they had cut from the fields. Those who went in front and those who followed were shouting: "Hosanna! BLESSED IS HE WHO COMES IN THE NAME OF THE LORD" (Mark 11:1-9).

I'm sure you picked up on the repetition of one particular word in that short reading. Yes, it was the word 'colt,' used for a young donkey. Although we all imagine it to be true, the Bible doesn't actually tell us that Mary, pregnant with Jesus, rode on a donkey into Bethlehem. But Mark here does tell us that Jesus rode on a donkey into Jerusalem. More accurately, it was a colt, the foal of a donkey. But why does Mark keep repeating the word 'colt'? He wants to catch our attention, and ring some bells, as we say. That is, he wants us to recall a text from the Old Testament. Here it is ...

"Rejoice greatly, O daughter of Zion! Shout in triumph, O daughter of Jerusalem! Behold, your king is coming to you; He is just and endowed with salvation, Humble, and mounted on a donkey, Even on a colt, the foal of a donkey" (Zechariah 9:9).

Even as Jesus' birth was predicted to be in Bethlehem, his arrival into Jerusalem where he would die, was also predicted. The crowds shouted out their 'hosannas.' The idea contained in this word is 'salvation.' God's King had arrived to save them! The mood would soon change, however. Jesus' first public words at Jerusalem are laden with judgement.

In Warren Wiersbe's *Meet Yourself in the Psalms*, he tells about a frontier town where a horse bolted and ran away with a wagon carrying a little boy. Seeing the child in danger, a young man risked his life to catch the horse and stop the wagon. The child who was saved grew up to become a lawless man, and one day he stood before a judge to be sentenced for a serious crime. The prisoner recognized the judge as the man who, years before had saved his life; so he pled for mercy on the basis of that experience. But the words from the bench silenced his plea: "Young man, then I was your saviour; today I am your judge, and I must sentence you to be hanged."

I'm reminded of that illustration as I read Mark's account of what is generally referred to as Jesus' triumphal entry into Jerusalem, where he was to die within a week. And he would die in exactly the way he has been repeatedly foretelling to his disciples. Jesus was greeted as a saviour but he quickly turned to judge the situation he had entered into. By this I mean that he famously entered the temple and overturned the tables of those who exchanged money there for animals to be sacrificed. This wasn't because it wasn't appropriate in itself, but there was corruption involved. It was, for some, a way of making money for themselves out of legitimate temple business.

Mark has also noted for us the fact that Jesus was deliberately using a form of words from the Old Testament. The words Jesus quoted described the temple as a den of robbers. Mark wants us to register that this has a certain context in the writing of the prophet Jeremiah:

TAKE YOUR MARK'S GOSPEL

> *"Will you steal, murder, and commit adultery and swear falsely, and offer sacrifices to Baal and walk after other gods that you have not known, then come and stand before Me in this house, which is called by My name, and say, 'We are delivered!' - that you may do all these abominations? Has this house, which is called by My name, become a den of robbers in your sight? Behold, I, even I, have seen it," declares the LORD. "But go now to My place which was in Shiloh, where I made My name dwell at the first, and see what I did to it because of the wickedness of My people Israel"* (Jeremiah 7:9-12).

And so we see the context. Jesus' use of the words 'den of robbers' in relation to the Jewish Temple resonated with the sense of God's impending judgement. They referred back to the desolation of the first place of worship which Joshua had located at Shiloh when the Israelites had come into the Promised Land at the first (Joshua 18:1). But they also served then as a warning that God was going to send the Babylonian armies to destroy his Temple which Solomon had built at Jerusalem. Jesus' message now ought to have been clear: by repeating this phrase, Jesus was sounding a warning that the days of this replacement Temple, known as Herod's Temple, were already numbered.

Perhaps Peter gets something of this significance – not only picked up from this phrase, but it may also have been the fact that Mark tells us Jesus cursed a fig tree at this time because of its barrenness. The very next day, Peter can't help noticing the fig tree cursed by Jesus had withered away. Does Peter now fear for the similar loss of the temple (as he'd just seen happen overnight with the fig tree)? Maybe he thinks, 'If a similar judgement should befall the Temple, what hope is there for us?' After all, at the dedication of that earlier Temple which had stood there, Solomon had asked God that his eyes would always be upon it to favour his people who prayed for help there, conscious of their sins (1 Kings 8:29). If the Temple was made desolate, where would they then get help, answers to prayer, and forgiveness?

The fig tree had represented the lack of return that God's people were bringing to God. They were just as barren, so under God's judgment. However, Jesus said that his followers should have faith in God. If so, as he had removed the fig tree, so mountainous difficulties could be removed by prayer. Access to God and forgiveness would not be withheld. Jesus, rather than any venerated site, is where we can meet with God.

For discussion:

1. How does Mark show that the Gospel is for those from all walks of life?
2. Rich and poor, saviour or judge, Mark presents us with contrasts – how do Acts 4:12 and 17:31 combine to disclose that we will meet Jesus as either saviour or judge?
3. A recent American survey revealed people's top concern was against corruption of officialdom. How does Jesus indicate history was repeating itself in terms of corruption in the very courts of God's temple at Jerusalem?
4. Pious Jews would associate the temple building with God's favour and forgiveness, a place to come to seek help from their God. How is Jesus reassuringly someone 'greater than the temple' (Matthew 12:6)?

CHAPTER ELEVEN: VARIOUS CONFLICTS IN THE TEMPLE COURTS

I think it's worth reminding ourselves that Mark began by announcing Jesus as God's son, the long-awaited king. He then went on to give different examples of the kind of authority we expect a divine king to have. Increasingly, at the end of Jesus' earthly life, this authority was openly and repeatedly questioned by one group after another hostile to Jesus.

Although Mark had opened his story by plainly affirming Jesus is the son of God, we've seen how some later said Jesus was mad or 'beside himself.' Many, today, would happily concede Jesus was a good man, but that's not an option - for as Jesus said to the rich ruler if he's good then he's God. If he's not good, then he's bad. The options then are mad, bad or God! As we explore together the endings of chapter 11 and chapter 12, we cannot fail to see that they confound the idea that Jesus was any kind of deranged conman. He is instead what Mark said in opening: the son of God.

One final point to rehearse as we begin to unpack the various conflicts that erupted in the temple courts – let's not lose sight of the incident where Jesus cursed a fig tree. We need to remember that an equally fruitless temple is under a curse. This temple is the scene for a series of challenges to Jesus' authority. First up is the conflict with temple authorities about authority (Mark 11:27-33):

> *"... as He was walking in the temple, the chief priests and the scribes and the elders came to Him, and began saying to Him, "By what authority are You doing these things, or who gave You this authority to do these things?" And Jesus said to them, "I will ask you one question, and you answer Me, and then I will tell you by what authority I do these things. "Was the baptism of John from heaven, or from men? Answer Me." They began reasoning among themselves, saying, "If we say, 'From heaven,' He will say, 'Then why did you not believe him?' "But shall we say, 'From men'?" - they were afraid of the people, for everyone considered John to have been a real prophet. Answering Jesus, they said, "We do not know." And Jesus said to them, "Nor will I tell you by what authority I do these things"* (Mark 11:27-33).

This is the first round of the contest. After the upsetting of the money-changing tables by Jesus, it seems some people had got more than a little upset themselves. They decided to set a trap for Jesus with a test question about the source of his authority. If Jesus answered that he was acting on personal heavenly authority, they would likely try to press blasphemy charges; if, on the other hand, he said his was mere earthly authority, they'd probably have pressed for criminal damage. But Jesus skilfully overturned the trap, just as he had done with the tables. It makes me think of a game of chess where if you threaten my king, the best defence is to defend by threatening yours. The masterful wisdom Jesus displayed in his answer is quite inconsistent with any allegation of madness.

John the Baptist, whom the Lord cited in his answer, is someone who features in the parable Jesus went on to speak to his opponents at the start of Mark chapter 12:

> *"And He began to speak to them in parables: "A man PLANTED A VINEYARD AND PUT A WALL AROUND IT, AND DUG A VAT UNDER THE WINE PRESS AND BUILT A TOWER, and rented it out to vine-growers and went on a journey. At the harvest time he sent a slave to the vine-growers, in order to receive some of the produce of the vineyard from the vine-growers. They took him, and beat him and sent him away empty-handed. Again he sent them another slave, and they wounded him in the head, and treated him shamefully. And he sent another, and that one they killed; and so with many others, beating some and killing others. He had one more to send, a beloved son; he sent him last of all to them, saying, 'They will respect my son.'*
>
> *But those vine-growers said to one another, 'This is the heir; come, let us kill him, and the inheritance will be ours!' They took him, and killed him and threw him out of the vineyard. What will the owner of the vineyard do? He will come and destroy the vine-growers, and will give the vineyard to others. Have you not even read this Scripture: 'THE STONE WHICH THE BUILDERS REJECTED, THIS BECAME THE CHIEF CORNER stone; THIS CAME ABOUT FROM THE LORD, AND IT IS MARVELOUS*

IN OUR EYES'?" And they were seeking to seize Him, and yet they feared the people, for they understood that He spoke the parable against them. And so they left Him and went away" (Mark 12:1-12).

The picture or analogy of comparing God's people, Israel, to a vineyard wasn't new. The prophet Isaiah had previously done the same in his Old Testament book. But it's now even worse than Isaiah had painted it in chapter 5 of his writings. In Isaiah's telling, the fruit produced was disappointingly low grade, but, in Jesus' updated version, the fruit is being wilfully withheld. There's an additional emotional build-up too in Jesus' story-telling, when we're told the owner decides to send not only his son, but his beloved son, and emphasizes that *surely* they will respect him.

It's all set up for the monstrous crime of the tenant farmers killing the son when he arrives to collect the proceeds. In his Gospel, Matthew, tells us (Matthew 21:41) that the tenants' crime – as depicted - so outrages the listeners that they bring in the verdict against them (shades of Nathan and David). This is just before the realization dawns on them that they've just condemned themselves out of their own mouths! What Jesus has done here is to explain his own death in terms of the nation's rebellion against God.

In the curious ending about a once rejected stone becoming the most important stone in the entire building – which seems to be about some kind of dramatic reversal of judgement, we sense that Jesus is talking about himself. They – the religious leaders, the nation-builders - were rejecting him and about to put him to death, but afterwards God would raise him up to the highest place – and that highest place would be in a (spiritual) temple that was designed to replace their now accursed temple. But, a rejected stone can never become the most important stone if that rejection involves death, not unless resurrection is involved. And that connects with a following topic - Jesus' conflict with the religious sect of the Sadducees about the fact that death does not end all (Mark 12:18-27).

The conflicts seem to be coming in waves: Pharisees and Herodians, Sadducees and Scribes, then after the Herodians quiz Jesus about taxes, and he's famously answered "Render to Caesar the things that are Caesar's, and to God the things that are God's" there comes a different sort of question from a scribe acting on his own and speaking much more sincerely and reasonably for himself. He asked Jesus which was the greatest commandment in God's Law. The Lord's reply was once again memorable, as he summarized the whole Law in terms of loving the Lord our God and, in the second place, loving our neighbour.

If this was a boxing contest, Jesus has just won the first four rounds! And he now scores a knockout punch. I say that because he totally confounds his critics when he:

> *"... began to say, as He taught in the temple, "How is it that the scribes say that the Christ is the son of David? David himself said in the Holy Spirit, 'THE LORD SAID TO MY LORD, "SIT AT MY RIGHT HAND, UNTIL I PUT YOUR ENEMIES BENEATH YOUR FEET.'" David himself calls Him*

'Lord'; so in what sense is He his son?" And the large crowd enjoyed listening to Him" (Mark 12:35-37).

This revealed that the scribes' view of the 'son of David' was narrower than the one Bartimaeus the blind beggar had. What an irony that was! Jesus ends with a damning critique of the religion of the scribes which was all about externals – how to look good in the eyes of others without dealing with inner corruption such as seizing widows' houses.

Unsurprisingly, Mark then spotlights a poor widow woman whom Jesus observed coming to the temple at that moment to give her contribution which was a mere cent. It was a negligible gift in the eyes of most (if not all) present, had they at least known about it, but in the eyes of the only one who mattered it was truly appreciated. This was a case of little being more than much, for, as Jesus said, she'd put in the offering box 'all she had to live on,' while the other rich donors had tossed in out of their surplus. Jesus noticed what this widow gave, but they hardly noticed the loss of what they themselves had given.

These answers Jesus gave at this time were interspersed with warnings of future judgement running through them like a thread. This, as we'll see, is a prelude to the next chapter (Mark 13).

For discussion:

1. What incidents in Jesus' recorded life would demonstrate that his was not the life of a deranged conman?
2. In the parable Jesus tells, can you identify (as reference points, see v.12) the Israel nation, its leaders, God's prophets and son? What was to happen after Jesus' death?
3. Mark is showcasing Jesus' authority in support of his opening claim to be God's son. Challenges to his authority intensify, but his answers always amaze. What was different about the scribe's question in v.28?
4. We may have questions and doubts, how may we become self-aware of our motivation?

CHAPTER TWELVE: THE END OF THE TEMPLE AND MUCH MORE

Mark at this point, his thirteenth chapter, has arrived within the last week of Jesus' life on earth: the week that lies between so-called 'Palm Sunday,' which saw his entrance into Jerusalem - when he was greeted with 'hosannas' - and a week later, the 'Resurrection Sunday.' During that week between those two Sundays, Jesus has been talking about judgement, a fig tree and the Jerusalem temple. At the beginning of chapter 13, we find Jesus' disciples also remarking about the temple:

> *"As He was going out of the temple, one of His disciples said to Him, "Teacher, behold what wonderful stones and what wonderful buildings!" And Jesus said to him, "Do you see these great buildings? Not one stone will be left upon another which will not be torn down." As He was sitting on the Mount of Olives opposite the temple, Peter and James and John and Andrew were questioning Him privately, "Tell us, when will these things be, and what will be the sign when all these things are going to be fulfilled?"* (Mark 13:1-4).

Mark presents the disciples' interest as specifically being about the end of the temple. And on this point, Jesus' words in Mark's gospel were fulfilled about 40 years later. This was when, responding to a revolt by Jewish Zealots, Emperor Nero commissioned Vespasian and his son Titus, to end the uprising.

From 66 until 70 AD, Jerusalem and the surrounding area was plagued by war which laid the city bare; destroying both it and its Temple.

Matthew, in his Gospel account of the same incident, phrases the questions asked more generally as being about the sign of the Lord's coming and the end of the age. This helps us to see there's a broader aspect to Jesus' answer - even the one given here - than simply being about what transpired in first century history. History, or should we say prophecy, was destined to repeat itself. Anyone who's looked at other examples of Bible prophecy will be aware of this phenomenon, but let's give one example by turning to Isaiah 7:14-16:

> *"Therefore the Lord Himself will give you a sign: Behold, a virgin will be with child and bear a son, and she will call His name Immanuel. He will eat curds and honey at the time He knows enough to refuse evil and choose good. For before the boy will know enough to refuse evil and choose good, the land whose two kings you dread will be forsaken"* (Isaiah 7:14-16).

When first spoken, this was directed primarily at the then king, Ahaz. He was the king of southern Israel, and his difficulty was that northern Israel and Syria had joined together in opposition to him. The sign in question - one which he received - concerned a female who was a virgin at the time when Isaiah spoke his message, but she would soon marry and have a baby. That boy would still be young when the Syrian-northern Israel alliance would come to be broken. That then was the contemporary fulfilment of the prophecy, which pinpointed a name and a designated timescale, but centuries later, the Holy Spirit led Matthew to quote the same prophecy (Isaiah 7:14) as a statement that was also true of a genuine virgin birth (i.e., a birth to a woman who was still a virgin). This is the first of many prophecies referring to Jesus Christ given by Isaiah around 700 years ahead of his birth. We can treat Mark chapter 13 in the same twofold way: with a partial fulfilment in the 40 years that followed Jesus speaking, but with the main fulfilment still to happen. Let's read on:

> "And Jesus began to say to them, "See to it that no one misleads you. Many will come in My name, saying, 'I am He!' and will mislead many. When you hear of wars and rumors of wars, do not be frightened; those things must take place; but that is not yet the end. For nation will rise up against nation, and kingdom against kingdom; there will be earthquakes in various places; there will also be famines. These things are merely the beginning of birth pangs.
>
> But be on your guard; for they will deliver you to the courts, and you will be flogged in the synagogues, and you will stand before governors and kings for My sake, as a testimony to them. The gospel must first be preached to all the nations. When they arrest you and hand you over, do not worry beforehand about what you are to say, but say whatever is given you in that hour; for it is not you who speak, but it is the Holy Spirit. Brother will betray brother to death, and a fa-

ther his child; and children will rise up against parents and have them put to death" (Mark 13:5-12).

Most of that had an application in the first century. Even some of what follows had a partial fulfilment then too ...

"You will be hated by all because of My name, but the one who endures to the end, he will be saved. But when you see the ABOMINATION OF DESOLATION standing where it should not be (let the reader understand), then those who are in Judea must flee to the mountains" (Mark 13:13-14).

Now here's where we find a big clue that this prophecy also referred to the 'end' of things that's still to come. This language is developed from the book of Daniel which states: *"His armed forces will rise up to desecrate the Temple fortress and will abolish the daily sacrifice. Then they will set up the abomination that causes desolation"* (Daniel 11:31). This was a prophecy that seemed to have found fulfilment in history during the Jewish struggle under a notorious persecutor by the name of Antiochus Epiphanes. The story is told (in 1 Maccabees 1.54ff) that they set up a desolating sacrilege at that time on the Jewish temple altar of burnt offering. When this 'abomination that causes desolation' disgraced the Temple in the past, it took the form of a pagan altar set up on the altar of God. It follows that Jesus, having this in his mind, was referring to an object that would disgrace the Temple once again at the time when it was nearing its destruction.

But, rather than just being about past history, and also about the disciples' *near future*, this prophecy is also about a *yet-to-be fulfilled future*. Jesus' statements were fulfilled in regard to the destruction under the invading Romans in the first century; however, the most important aspects of his prophecy were *not* fulfilled in the destruction in AD 70. In order to show the difference, I want to draw your attention to two clues, both found in Mark 13:14. The first is the wording, 'let the reader understand.' This implies there was a meaning for later readers of Mark's Gospel, and not only a meaning for Jesus' immediate hearers. Then there are the words 'when you see.' Whom do they refer to? To find out, we need to read on.

> *"For those days will be a time of tribulation such as has not occurred since the beginning of the creation which God created until now, and never will"* (Mark 13:19).

Please note the words: 'those days will be a time of tribulation' ... Now let's read further:

> *"But in those days, after that tribulation, THE SUN WILL BE DARKENED AND THE MOON WILL NOT GIVE ITS LIGHT, AND THE STARS WILL BE FALLING from heaven, and the powers that are in the heavens will be shaken. Then they will see THE SON OF MAN COMING IN CLOUDS with great power and glory ... Truly I say to you, this generation will not pass away until all these things take place"* (Mark 13:24-26,30).

The intriguing question is: 'which generation does Jesus refer to?' The only answer that can be given in context is that it has to refer to the generation who see the days of tribulation. And this means 'tribulation' with a capital T, for Jesus said it would be unprecedented in its ferocity. For future Jewish believers whose trust is in Jesus as Messiah, rescue comes in the form of the 'Son of Man coming in clouds' (v.26). Once again, this 'Son of Man' language is taken from the book of Daniel. Jesus did not return in AD 70, so it now becomes clear that the first century Fall of Jerusalem and the coming of the Son of Man are separated in time, as two fulfilments of the same prophecy.

Other Bible passages, such as the ending of the book of the prophet Zechariah, predict the Messiah, Jesus, described as the pierced one (Zechariah 12:10), returning to this earth at a time when the city of Jerusalem has again been a burdensome stone to many nations (Zechariah 12:3) at the end of history. Faithful Jews, in their beleaguered city, are rescued from something worse still than the Holocaust, when Jesus returns as 'son of Man' (Zechariah 14:2,3).

> *"Now learn the parable from the fig tree: when its branch has already become tender and puts forth its leaves, you know that summer is near. Even so, you too, when you see these things happening, recognize that He is near, right at the door"* (Mark 13:28-29).

The parable of the fig tree signals the truthfulness of Jesus' words. The fig tree as it begins to bloom indicates that summer will come soon. The generation that sees these signs can equally know the return of Jesus to this earth will be soon, and they will also see it. The parable of the fig tree may also look back to the earlier cursed fig tree in chapter 11. That tree had only leaves and was cursed because it bore no fruit. It stood for the Temple and its custodians. But this other mention of a fig tree is preparing for a time when there will be a future harvest – blessing for some; judgement for others when Jesus returns as promised.

For discussion:

1. It's important to look for clues to discover when a prophecy applies. What was different between the two clear fulfilments of the one prophecy in Isaiah 7:14?
2. This chapter is recognized as being difficult to interpret correctly (and commentators vary). What's the significance for our understanding of the two clues found in v.14?
3. The expressions 'synagogues' (v.9); 'the abomination of desolation'; 'those in Judea' (v.14); and 'Son of Man' (v.26); all have a strong Jewish association in the Bible. We believe, therefore, this is the Lord returning to Israel. For whom do you think he will return in John 14:3 and 1 Thessalonians 4:13-18?
4. Are you ready for Jesus' return for his Church? (Note 1 Thessalonians 5:9 affirming we will not go through the tribulation of this chapter).

CHAPTER THIRTEEN: RECLINING AT TABLE

I recall once hearing about a Chinese guy who proposed to his girlfriend inside a heart-shaped collection of no less than 99 boxed and brand-new iPhones that he'd bought for $94,000 dollars in order to make an impression. Sadly, for him, it didn't. And I never did see the logic of it, but it was presumably intended as a lavish, if misguided, way to show his devotion. In a moment, as we read in Mark's Gospel we'll encounter an unforgettably lavish expression of devotion that will be eternally appreciated.

Meals out can be enjoyable, and sometimes even dramatic. In chapter 14, Mark takes us to two dinner parties with a difference. At one Jesus is adored; and at the other, he's betrayed. This is the way Mark introduces us to the events surrounding Jesus' death. Could it be that even in these contrasting meal table settings, we're meant to begin to realize that Jesus' death forces us all to take sides. But let's not be late in joining the first dinner party ...

> *"Now the Passover and Unleavened Bread were two days away; and the chief priests and the scribes were seeking how to seize Him by stealth and kill Him; for they were saying, "Not during the festival, otherwise there might be a riot of the people." While He was in Bethany at the home of Simon the leper, and reclining at the table, there came a woman with an alabaster vial of very costly perfume of pure nard; and she broke*

the vial and poured it over His head. But some were indignantly remarking to one another, "Why has this perfume been wasted? "For this perfume might have been sold for over three hundred denarii, and the money given to the poor." And they were scolding her.

But Jesus said, "Let her alone; why do you bother her? She has done a good deed to Me. For you always have the poor with you, and whenever you wish you can do good to them; but you do not always have Me. She has done what she could; she has anointed My body beforehand for the burial. Truly I say to you, wherever the gospel is preached in the whole world, what this woman has done will also be spoken of in memory of her." Then Judas Iscariot, who was one of the twelve, went off to the chief priests in order to betray Him to them. They were glad when they heard this, and promised to give him money. And he began seeking how to betray Him at an opportune time" (Mark 14:1-11).

Mark sprinkles this chapter with references to the Jewish Feast of Passover (in vv.1,12,16). The Jewish Feast of Passover commemorated the time when God, by the hand of Moses, rescued his people from their slavery in the land of Egypt. As well as an actual historical event, the Bible writers treat it as an analogy for other times of God's deliverance. In particular, it was the prototype of a greater rescue that someone greater than Moses would bring about. But more on that later, for we need to get back to the first special mealtime in Mark 14.

It was held at Bethany, and John, in his Gospel, reminds us this is where Lazarus and his sisters lived. Lazarus, we remember, was the man whom Jesus raised from the dead. Mark's interest isn't about the menu, but the meal was significant for something sensational that happened during it. A woman – John tells us that it was Mary – took a jar containing very expensive perfume and broke it and poured the perfume over Jesus, over his head. The guests complained about the sheer extravagance of this act. The value of this perfume which was an aromatic oil from an East Indian plant was roughly speaking a year's wages. Think of that!

In the United Kingdom a recent estimate of the average yearly salary is in the region of twenty-seven thousand pounds! This woman didn't hold back. She broke the container, and she broke the bank, as she poured all the fragrant contents out so lavishly upon Jesus. The Lord Jesus appreciated it – he really appreciated it. He wasn't someone to hold anything back: his surrender of himself to the will of God at the cross ensured that God's love is lavished on every one of us (1 John 3:1) who takes Jesus as our personal savior, our rescuer from the slavery of the guilt of our sinful habits and practices.

But then the spotlight falls on another individual guest at the meal table. Elsewhere (in John's Gospel) we read he was the one to give us the valuation of the worth of the perfume - but only offered by way of criticism, saying it would have been better given to help poor people. Not that Judas – for he's the speaker at this point – wished to help the poor, but only to have opportunity to divert it into his own pocket (see John 12:6). Later, we'll discover his true evaluation of Jesus was thirty silver coins, the price of a mere slave. Even as Jesus defends the woman's actions in terms of preparing him for burial; Judas slips away from the meal with the decision now firm in his mind that he wants to betray Jesus.

He went to the chief priests who'd been thinking that the festival time was not the best of times to act against Jesus. But let's repeat what we said earlier: Mark sprinkles this chapter with references to the Jewish Feast of Passover. What an irony! Those who are plotting to take Jesus' life had rejected this date in their fickle plans; but Mark is revealing how Jesus was in control of his own destiny, in full accord with God's sovereign will. Jesus, the ultimate Passover sacrifice, was scheduled to die at this time. The religious leaders who are the plotters against Jesus are grateful for Judas' offer to betray Jesus and are now waiting for an opportunity, as yet still uncertain of exactly when. On the other hand, Jesus knows this, and has his plans already made, as the disciples discover ...

> *"On the first day of Unleavened Bread, when the Passover lamb was being sacrificed, His disciples said to Him, "Where do You want us to go and prepare for You to eat the Passover?" And He sent two of His disciples and said to them, "Go into the city, and a man will meet you carrying a pitcher of water; follow him; and wherever he enters, say to the owner of the house, 'The Teacher says, "Where is My guest room in which I may eat the Passover with My disciples?"' And he himself will show you a large upper room furnished and ready; prepare for us there." The disciples went out and*

> *came to the city, and found it just as He had told them; and they prepared the Passover.*
>
> *When it was evening He came with the twelve. As they were reclining at the table and eating, Jesus said, "Truly I say to you that one of you will betray Me - one who is eating with Me." They began to be grieved and to say to Him one by one, "Surely not I?" And He said to them, "It is one of the twelve, one who dips with Me in the bowl. For the Son of Man is to go just as it is written of Him; but woe to that man by whom the Son of Man is betrayed! It would have been good for that man if he had not been born"* (Mark 14:12-21).

This now is the second 'dinner party' or more properly the annual religious meal of roast lamb – the Passover Lamb commemoration. The feel we get from Mark is that everything is under control. It's similar to Jesus' entrance into the city of Jerusalem, the previous Sunday. At that time, you remember, he had foreseen the disciples finding a colt, the foal of a donkey, for his use. Again, it's all anticipated: the disciples go and meet, as predicted, a man carrying a water jar who directs them to a room already furnished and ready. It's there that Jesus sits down for this very special meal with his disciples, the Twelve.

For the second time in the opening verses of Mark chapter 14, Jesus is again 'reclining at table.' This was, of course, the table etiquette in those days, as we might have learnt from our Latin or history classes at school. We're told that to sit bolt upright is best, but in those days, they reclined at table. This was long before fast food was invented - meals were more leisurely! Now if the adoring woman was singled out at the first meal occasion, this time it's Judas, the betrayer, who's singled out. However, what follows is far more important:

> *"While they were eating, He took some bread, and after a blessing He broke it, and gave it to them, and said, "Take it; this is My body." And when He had taken a cup and given thanks, He gave it to them, and they all drank from it. And He said to them, "This is My blood of the covenant, which is poured out for many. "Truly I say to you, I will never again drink of the fruit of the vine until that day when I drink it new in the kingdom of God"* (Mark 14:22-25).

If ever there was a shock announcement at a meal table, this was it. When Jesus took bread and announced: *'this is my body,'* he was identifying himself with the ultimate sacrifice that had long been pictured in the Passover lamb. Christ, our Passover, was to die for our sins (1 Corinthians 5:7; 1 Corinthians 15:3). As an evaluation, £27,000 now seems cheap. Isaac Watts in his hymn puts it well – 'Were the whole realm of nature mine that were an offering far too small.'

For discussion:

1. Mark has been bringing side by side rich and poor; saviour and judge; and now acts of adoration and betrayal. Which side are you on? Why?
2. As with his mode of entrance into Jerusalem, so now with the choice of venue for the Jewish Passover Commemoration: Jesus details in advance what his disciples will find. Why is Mark including this information, do you think?
3. Jesus' death was no accident, but why was the timing – at Passover - significant?
4. How are we to understand the meaning of 'Holy Communion,' the basis for which is recorded here?

CHAPTER FOURTEEN: BETRAYED, DENIED AND VERY ALONE

We're about to arrive at the moment Jesus had been preparing his disciples for all along. As they leave the meal-table where we left them last time, Jesus tells them: "You will all fall away, because it is written, 'I WILL STRIKE DOWN THE SHEPHERD, AND THE SHEEP SHALL BE SCATTERED' (Mark 14:27).

Quoting an Old Testament's prophet's words, and applying them to himself, Jesus again predicts his death - or at least, he infers that God is about to strike him. He's the shepherd, and his disciples are the sheep, his followers. They're the ones who'll be scattered. The striking and the scattering, taken together here, set the twin themes of this section, and they're interwoven, of course. Mark then writes - and if this was all from Peter's memoirs, as most believe – then this would have been a painful recollection for Peter.

> *"Peter said to Him, "Even though all may fall away, yet I will not." And Jesus said to him, "Truly I say to you, that this very night, before a rooster crows twice, you yourself will deny Me three times." But Peter kept saying insistently, "Even if I have to die with You, I will not deny You!" And they all were saying the same thing also"* (Mark 14:29-31).

Not only did Jesus know in advance that he was going to be struck by God, he also knew he'd be abandoned by his disciples. Back at the meal-table, if the disciples had been confused, now they were indignant. If they'd been confused about which one of them Jesus was referring to as the betrayer; now they were indignant that he was saying they'd all abandon him. This section of Mark's Gospel we're considering lies between the promise and the fulfilment of the denial by Peter. He was the most vocal of the disciples in protesting his loyalty (vv.30 and 72). Yes, the focus is certainly on Peter. Ok, moving on ... Peter had boasted that he was ready, if necessary, to die with Jesus, but soon we find he can't even stay awake and be supportive while Jesus is at prayer:

> *"They came to a place named Gethsemane; and He said to His disciples, "Sit here until I have prayed." And He took with Him Peter and James and John, and began to be very distressed and troubled. And He said to them, "My soul is deeply grieved to the point of death; remain here and keep watch." And He went a little beyond them, and fell to the ground and began to pray that if it were possible, the hour might pass Him by. And He was saying, "Abba! Father! All things are possible for You; remove this cup from Me; yet not what I will, but what You will"* (Mark 14:32-36).

It's hard not to notice the different attitude Jesus shows to this danger. In the midst of the storm on the Sea of Galilee he'd remained asleep until awakened by the panicked disciples. At that point he calmly rose up and stilled the storm with a word of command. Now in the Garden of Gethsemane, he's greatly distressed as he anticipates the experience that lies ahead which he styles as a 'cup' he must drink. This is an idea often used in the first part of the Bible (Isaiah 51:17-23; Jeremiah 25:15-29; Ezekiel 23:31-34; Habbakuk 2:15-16) – where such a 'cup' pictures God's judgement being served in this way to various nations that were hostile to God's ancient people of Israel.

> *"And He came and found them sleeping, and said to Peter, "Simon, are you asleep? Could you not keep watch for one hour?"* (Mark 14:37).

This happened not once, but three times, each time that Jesus returned from praying. But now it gets worse. If they've gone from bravado to slumber, next we find them going from slumber to flight, that is, running away …

> *"Immediately while He was still speaking, Judas, one of the twelve, came up accompanied by a crowd with swords and clubs, who were from the chief priests and the scribes and the elders. Now he who was betraying Him had given them a signal, saying, "Whomever I kiss, He is the one; seize Him and lead Him away under guard." After coming, Judas immediately went to Him, saying, "Rabbi!" and kissed Him. They laid hands on Him and seized Him. But one of those who stood by drew his sword, and struck the slave of the high priest and cut off his ear.*
>
> *And Jesus said to them, "Have you come out with swords and clubs to arrest Me, as you would against a*

robber? Every day I was with you in the temple teaching, and you did not seize Me; but this has taken place to fulfill the Scriptures." And they all left Him and fled. A young man was following Him, wearing nothing but a linen sheet over his naked body; and they seized him. But he pulled free of the linen sheet and escaped naked" (Mark 14:43-52).

Jesus is left all alone (see especially v.50). By saying that all this was happening to fulfil the Bible's prophecies, it seems as if Jesus effectively ended any resistance by his disciples and surrendered himself to the mob led by Judas, the betrayer. At this, it's as if the penny finally drops for the disciples. In other words, they realize that he really means all he's been saying – it's for real that he's going to die. At this, they flee.

"They led Jesus away to the high priest; and all the chief priests and the elders and the scribes gathered together. Peter had followed Him at a distance, right into the courtyard of the high priest; and he was sitting with the officers and warming himself at the fire. Now the chief priests and the whole Council kept trying to obtain testimony against Jesus to put Him to death, and they were not finding any. For many were giving false testimony against Him, but their testimony was not consistent. Some stood up and began to give false testimony against Him, saying, "We heard Him say, 'I will destroy this temple made with hands, and in three days I will build another made without hands.'"

Not even in this respect was their testimony consistent" (Mark 14:53-59).

It's as if Mark wants us to be really clear that this was a sham trial. He uses a lot of repetition about it being false testimony and testimony that wasn't consistent. Of course, it wasn't: for only the truth is coherent. Then …

> *"The high priest stood up and came forward and questioned Jesus, saying, "Do You not answer? … Again the high priest was questioning Him, and saying to Him, "Are You the Christ, the Son of the Blessed One?" And Jesus said, "I am …"* (Mark 14:60-62).

And that was what condemned him in their minds, it was this: his claim to deity. That's when those religious men decided a death sentence was in order to end the most beautiful life the planet has ever seen. And it was then that all the hateful physical abuse began. Throughout the trial, we see Jesus composed under cross-examination by Israel's high priest. What a contrast Mark now makes as he switches in parallel to another trial. It's the test Peter was undergoing in the courtyard of the high priest. Peter had at least followed at a distance, and anyone reading for the first time may wonder if there'll be a flicker of hope – will the disciples be found to be in complete and utter disarray or will Peter salvage a little of the reputation of the disciples?

> *"As Peter was below in the courtyard, one of the servant-girls of the high priest came, and seeing Peter warming himself, she looked at him and said, "You*

also were with Jesus the Nazarene." But he denied it, saying, "I neither know nor understand what you are talking about." And he went out onto the porch. The servant-girl saw him, and began once more to say to the bystanders, "This is one of them!" But again he denied it. And after a little while the bystanders were again saying to Peter, "Surely you are one of them, for you are a Galilean too." But he began to curse and swear, "I do not know this man you are talking about!" Immediately a rooster crowed a second time. And Peter remembered how Jesus had made the remark to him, "Before a rooster crows twice, you will deny Me three times." And he began to weep" (Mark 14:66-72).

Peter crumbles under a chat with a servant-girl. He didn't deny himself, but he denied Jesus. Before we criticize, however, we must face the fact that we're very often so like Peter – it happens every time we fail to speak up for the truth about Jesus.

For discussion:

1. Why would Jesus refer to his death as God striking him?
2. Was the root of the disciples' failure here their failure to pray? How might it have made a difference for them? Are there times we look back to and regret not praying?
3. Do you think it might have been Jesus' non-resistance that was the final reality check for the disciples? Was this the point when their intention to die with him was abandoned?
4. What was the charge against Jesus ultimately?
5. Have there been any times when we can identify with Peter in his denials?

CHAPTER FIFTEEN: THE KING WHO STUMBLED TO HIS THRONE

Yes, the king who stumbled to his throne. In our review of the life of Jesus, as given us in Mark's Gospel, we come to the day Jesus was crucified. Here we find that the more undignified and harsh the treatment they inflict on him, the more compelling is his dignified response.

> *"Early in the morning the chief priests with the elders and scribes and the whole Council, immediately held a consultation; and binding Jesus, they led Him away and delivered Him to Pilate. Pilate questioned Him, "Are You the King of the Jews?" And He answered him, "It is as you say." The chief priests began to accuse Him harshly. Then Pilate questioned Him again, saying, "Do You not answer? See how many charges they bring against You!" But Jesus made no further answer; so Pilate was amazed"* (Mark 15:1-5).

Jesus' quiet composure, even his silence at times, amazed the governor, as it had the high priest earlier. Pilate, the Roman governor, asked a similar question to one we've heard the high priest ask previously. The high priest had asked: *"Are you the Christ, the Son of the Blessed One?"* (Mark 14:61). We've said before that the meaning of 'Christ' is the 'Anointed One,' in the sense of God's anointed king. The royal identity of Jesus as king is something we trace right throughout this section of the Gospel.

> *"Now at the feast he [Pilate] used to release for them any one prisoner whom they requested. The man named Barabbas had been imprisoned with the insurrectionists who had committed murder in the insurrection. The crowd went up and began asking him to do as he had been accustomed to do for them. Pilate answered them, saying, "Do you want me to release for you the King of the Jews?" For he was aware that the chief priests had handed Him over because of envy. But the chief priests stirred up the crowd to ask him to release Barabbas for them instead.*
>
> *Answering again, Pilate said to them, "Then what shall I do with Him whom you call the King of the Jews?" They shouted back, "Crucify Him!" But Pilate said to them, "Why, what evil has He done?" But they shouted all the more, "Crucify Him!" Wishing to satisfy the crowd, Pilate released Barabbas for them, and after having Jesus scourged, he handed Him over to be crucified"* (Mark 15:6-15).

Twice, again, Mark records Pilate describing Jesus as 'the King of the Jews.' In addition, we have introduced to us the idea of Jesus, the man who is innocent of all charges, being substituted effectively for a man who was truly guilty, even Barabbas.

> *"The soldiers took Him away into the palace (that is, the Praetorium), and they called together the whole*

Roman cohort. They dressed Him up in purple, and after twisting a crown of thorns, they put it on Him; and they began to acclaim Him, "Hail, King of the Jews!" They kept beating His head with a reed, and spitting on Him, and kneeling and bowing before Him. After they had mocked Him, they took the purple robe off Him and put His own garments on Him. And they led Him out to crucify Him" (Mark 15:16-20).

Again, in sarcastic mockery now, Jesus is addressed as the King of the Jews. Picking up on this theme we've detected, I'd like to insert here an imaginary account of a later recollection Pilate is imagined to have had of the events of the day of Jesus' crucifixion:

"The clerk began reading the absurd list of charges, the priestly delegations punctuating these with the palm rubbings, the beard strokings, the eye rollings, and the pious gutturals – by now which I had learned to ignore, but I more felt it, Gaius, than heard it. I questioned him mechanically and he answered very little. But what he said and the way he said it – it was as if his level gaze had pulled up my naked soul right up into my eyes and was probing me there and a voice kept saying in my ears "Why, you're on trial, Pilate!" ...

I appealed to the crowd, hoping that they would be his sympathisers, but [the high priest] had stationed agitators to whip up the beasts that cry for blood. And you know how in this town here any citizen loves the blood of another person just after breakfast and screams for another's blood. I had him beaten, Gaius, a thorough barracks-room beating. I'm still not sure why. To appease the crowd, I guess ...

Well, it didn't work, Gaius. The crowd roared like some slavering beast when I brought him back. If only you could've watched Him - they had thrown some rags of mock purple over his ... bleeding shoulders. They'd jammed a chaplet of thorns down on his forehead and it fitted. It all fitted, Gaius. He stood there watching them from my balcony, swaying from weakness by now, but royal, I tell you, not just pain, but pity shining from his eyes and I kept thinking somehow this is monstrous - this is upside down. That purple is real. That crown is real and somehow these animal noises the crowd is shrieking should be praise and then [the high priest] played his masterstroke on me - he announced there in public that this Jesus claimed a crown and that was treason to Caesar. And the guards began to glance at one another quickly and that mob of spineless fools began to shout, "Hail Caesar, Hail Caesar" and, Gaius, I knew I was beaten - I gave the order. I couldn't look at him ..."

We stress again that was only someone's imagination, but if Pilate did feel that he was on trial that day, it would have been accurate - and it's the same for us all as we read this. Whether or not we actually believe the claims of Christ the King is what will finally judge us. All who don't believe are judged already. Returning to the biblical text of Mark's Gospel now:

> *"They pressed into service a passer-by coming from the country, Simon of Cyrene (the father of Alexander and Rufus), to bear His cross. Then they brought Him to the place Golgotha, which is translated, Place of*

a Skull ... It was the third hour when they crucified Him. The inscription of the charge against Him read, "THE KING OF THE JEWS." They crucified two robbers with Him, one on His right and one on His left ... Those passing by were hurling abuse at Him, wagging their heads, and saying, "Ha! You who are going to destroy the temple and rebuild it in three days, save Yourself, and come down from the cross!"

In the same way the chief priests also, along with the scribes, were mocking Him among themselves and saying, "He saved others; He cannot save Himself." Let this Christ, the King of Israel, now come down from the cross, so that we may see and believe!" Those who were crucified with Him were also insulting Him" (Mark 15:21-22, 25-27, 29-32).

The reference to the inscription, and the sneer of the priests and scribes, continue the single thread we're tracing: of Jesus' kingship being emphasized by Mark.

"When the sixth hour came, darkness fell over the whole land until the ninth hour. At the ninth hour Jesus cried out with a loud voice, "ELOI, ELOI, LAMA SABACHTHANI?" which is translated, "MY GOD, MY GOD, WHY HAVE YOU FORSAKEN ME?" ... And Jesus uttered a loud cry, and breathed His last. And the veil of the temple was torn in two from top to bottom. When the centurion, who was standing right in front of Him, saw the way He breathed His last,

he said, "Truly this man was the Son of God!" (Mark 15:33-34, 37-39).

And so we arrive at the third confession of Jesus as the son of God. At the beginning of our remarks on this Gospel, we said this whole Gospel was framed and divided by three similar confessions at its beginning, middle and end.

You'll recall our comment that Jesus knew all along the timing of his death. We've remarked how the details of his entry to Jerusalem, and of the venue for the last supper meal, were all under his control. Even when the conspirators were saying 'not at the feast,' Jesus knew that was the appointed hour. Why? Because it was 'Passover time.' It was the time for the ultimate sacrifice – of which the annual ritual had only ever been a pointer. By dying, Jesus drank the cup of judgement from his father's hand – the cup he so much dreaded as he entered Gethsemane's Garden. The judgement of those three supernaturally darkened hours, marked by the equally supernatural ripping of the temple curtain, was suffered by one whose royal dignity was never in question, but finally affirmed by the Roman centurion. He, our royal substitute, our sacrificial lamb, paid there the price of our human rebellion, so that the judgement due to us might forever 'pass over' us instead.

For discussion:

1. We've suggested that Pilate may have felt that he – the judge – was being judged himself that day. In what sense is it true that how we judge what happened then will ultimately be what judges us in the end (see John 3:18)?
2. In what ways does Jesus' dignified composure while suffering harsh injustice impress you?
3. What is the added and over-riding dimension to this suffering? Try to pick up on and involve terms such as 'substitute'; 'passover lamb'; and 'the cup' (of divine judgement).
4. Have you ever made a confession like the centurion, expressing heartfelt gratitude to the Lord?

CHAPTER SIXTEEN: THE MOST IMPORTANT PRESS RELEASE IN HISTORY

Someone rising from the dead was a phenomenon just as unthinkable to the minds of Jesus' first followers as it seems to ours today. Don't assume naïve earliest followers of Christ superstitiously nodded through the story of Jesus' claimed resurrection. But, eventually, even the most hesitant among them did find the resurrected Christ a reality that they simply couldn't deny. And they went to their deaths talking about it, spreading the news around the world for 2,000 years.

Sceptics say they'll only believe a miracle if the alternative is even more unbelievable. By the sceptic's own test the resurrection is the lesser miracle of the two – and the one to be believed. The alternative is that these early devotees were hoaxing it – and doing it entirely consistently for decades - and ultimately they (pretty much all of that core group) were prepared to give their lives for something they allegedly knew was only a lie. That's harder to believe, is it not? Take the testimony of Chuck Colson on that point.

Chuck Colson was someone who pled guilty to a single charge of obstructing justice in return for telling all he knew about Watergate. Remember, Watergate was a major political scandal that occurred in the United States in the 1970s, following a break-in at the Democratic National Committee (DNC) headquarters at the Watergate office complex in Washington, D.C. and President Richard Nixon's administration's attempted cover-up of its involvement. When this was investigated by the U.S. Congress, their resistance led to a constitutional crisis. That was when Chuck Colson, who was embroiled in this conspiracy, accepted a plea-bargain. Later he said: 'I know the resurrection is a fact ... Watergate proved it to me ... Watergate embroiled 12 of the most powerful men in the world ... and they couldn't keep a lie for three weeks ... You're telling me 12 apostles could keep a lie for 40 years? Absolutely impossible ...'

Let's now look at some of the facts, as Mark lays them out:

> *"There were also some women looking on from a distance, among whom were Mary Magdalene, and Mary the mother of James the Less and Joses, and Salome. When He was in Galilee, they used to follow Him and minister to Him; and there were many other women who came up with Him to Jerusalem. When evening had already come, because it was the preparation day, that is, the day before the Sabbath, Joseph of Arimathea came, a prominent member of the Council, who himself was waiting for the kingdom of God; and he gathered up courage and went in before Pilate, and asked for the body of Jesus. Pilate wondered if He was dead by this time, and summoning the centurion, he questioned him as to whether He was already dead.*
>
> *And ascertaining this from the centurion, he granted the body to Joseph. Joseph bought a linen cloth, took Him down, wrapped Him in the linen cloth and laid Him in a tomb which had been hewn out in the rock; and he rolled a stone against the entrance of the tomb.*

> *Mary Magdalene and Mary the mother of Joses were looking on to see where He was laid. When the Sabbath was over, Mary Magdalene, and Mary the mother of James, and Salome, bought spices, so that they might come and anoint Him. Very early on the first day of the week, they came to the tomb when the sun had risen"* (Mark 15:40-47, 16:1-2).

Thanks to Pilate checking the fact, we know Jesus was certified dead. That rules out the theory that tries to maintain Jesus had only swooned. Last time, we saw how Mark kept repeating references to Jesus as King of the Jews. In this final section under consideration, it now seems as if he's deliberately repeating the identities of these three women. Now why would he do that? It should make us think. For one thing, the unusual feature of duplicate listing of names in adjacent verses assures us that the women who saw the body placed in the tomb, were the exact same ones who returned to anoint it. Mark wants us to be sure there could have been no miscommunication about which tomb was the correct one to return to for the very same women were involved: so, the 'wrong tomb' theory is hopeless.

By the way, there's surely another reason why the women were the first witnesses. In the first century, the testimony of women wasn't counted as credible. Josephus, the first century Jewish historian, writes "But let not the testimony of women be admitted, on account of the levity and boldness of their sex ... since it is probable that they may not speak truth, either out of hope of gain, or fear of punishment." No man in the first century would give credence to a woman's testimony. Given that a woman's testimony was not credible, why would the gospel writers report them as witnesses, indeed, the *first* witnesses for the resurrection? Wouldn't it have made more sense to offer some credible, male testimonial?

Anglican priest and physicist John Polkinghorne answers this question with a resounding "No!" He writes: "Perhaps the strongest reason of taking the stories of the empty tomb absolutely seriously lies in the fact that it is women who play the leading role. It would have been very unlikely for anyone in the ancient world who was concocting a story to assign the principal part to women since, in those times, they were not considered capable of being reliable witnesses in a court of law. It is surely much more probable that they appear in the gospel accounts precisely because they actually fulfilled the role that the stories assign to them, and in so doing, they make a startling discovery."

> *"They were saying to one another, "Who will roll away the stone for us from the entrance of the tomb?" Looking up, they saw that the stone had been rolled away, although it was extremely large"* (Mark 16:3-4).

This also emphasizes multiple witnesses who described finding the unexpected. Out with the theory that says they were merely hallucinating, seeing only what they wanted.

> *"Entering the tomb, they saw a young man sitting at the right, wearing a white robe; and they were amazed. And he said to them, "Do not be amazed; you are looking for Jesus the Nazarene, who has been crucified. He has risen; He is not here; behold, here is*

> *the place where they laid Him. "But go, tell His disciples and Peter, 'He is going ahead of you to Galilee; there you will see Him, just as He told you.'" They went out and fled from the tomb, for trembling and astonishment had gripped them; and they said nothing to anyone, for they were afraid"* (Mark 16:5-8).

'Tell ... Peter,' what an authentic touch that is, relayed on behalf of someone who'd never break a crushed reed. And Peter was no doubt feeling crushed by his denials. Then, again, the mention of Galilee affirms exactly what the Lord himself had promised when predicting the scattering of his disciples. Now, let's continue the actual narrative with Mark:

> *"Afterward He appeared to the eleven themselves as they were reclining at the table; and He reproached them for their unbelief and hardness of heart, because they had not believed those who had seen Him after He had risen. And He said to them, "Go into all the world and preach the gospel to all creation ... So then, when the Lord Jesus had spoken to them, He was received up into heaven and sat down at the right hand of God. And they went out and preached everywhere ..."* (Mark 16:14-15,19-20).

Another dinner party – albeit it must have been a very solemn one. It was another case of 'reclining at table,' but this would turn out to be the best occasion of all! For Jesus appeared to them alive and well! And here's another touch of authenticity: they include the fact that he reproached them for their lack of faith.

Probably the most influential British philosopher of religion of the last half century is long-time Oxford professor Richard Swinburne. In 2003, he published a book entitled *The Resurrection of God Incarnate*, and in it he concludes that on the available evidence today, it is 97% probable that Jesus truly – miraculously - rose from the dead, proving that he is the God he claimed to be. Interesting that God should be alive and well in university philosophy departments of all places! Historians and lawyers (check out Thomas Arnold and Simon Greenleaf to name but two) have gone on record as saying that the resurrection of Jesus is the best attested fact in all of history.

The Apostle Paul preached *"Jesus and the resurrection"* (Acts 17:18). Why that emphasis? Because he taught (1 Corinthians 15:14) that *"if Christ has not been raised, then ... [the Christian] faith ... is vain."* The case for Christianity stands or falls on the objective reality of whether or not Christ was raised. Christianity cannot be of moderate importance: it is either of no importance (if Christ was not raised); or it is all-important (as Christ was indeed raised). The most personal and important question is: what is your response? Will it be like Andy Stanley's? 'If a man can predict his own death and resurrection, and pull it off, I just go with whatever that man says.' Or, like Eugene Petersen's? 'The Bible is not a script for a funeral service, but it is the record of God always bringing life where we expected to find death.'

For discussion:

1. What are some of the alternative theories for the empty tomb? (Note: Jesus' enemies at the time did not dispute that there was an empty tomb).
2. How does Mark's account help us to dispose of them one at a time?
3. What touches of authenticity could you detect, giving it the ring of truth?
4. Explain how Colson's Watergate analogy makes the face-value truthfulness of this account easier to believe than thinking of it as a mere fabrication (thus passing the sceptic's test)?
5. What is your response to the evidence (this is the biggest decision anyone can make)?

Did you love *Take Your Mark's Gospel*? Then you should read *Get Real ... Living Every Day as an Authentic Follower of Christ* by Brian Johnston!

Helpful, practical and scriptural guidance on Bible study, personal and collective prayer, worship, church life and family life, with the goal of becoming authentic, credible disciples who live with real integrity!

Also by Brian Johnston

Healthy Churches - God's Bible Blueprint For Growth
Hope for Humanity: God's Fix for a Broken World
First Corinthians: Nothing But Christ Crucified
Bible Answers to Listeners' Questions
Living in God's House: His Design in Action
Christianity 101: Seven Bible Basics
Nights of Old: Bible Stories of God at Work
Daniel Decoded: Deciphering Bible Prophecy
A Test of Commitment: 15 Challenges to Stimulate Your Devotion to Christ
John's Epistles - Certainty in the Face of Change
If Atheism Is True...
8 Amazing Privileges of God's People: A Bible Study of Romans 9:4-5
Learning from Bible Grandparents
Increasing Your Christian Footprint
Christ-centred Faith
Mindfulness That Jesus Endorses
Amazing Grace! Paul's Gospel Message to the Galatians
Abraham: Friend of God
The Future in Bible Prophecy
Unlocking Hebrews
Learning How To Pray - From the Lord's Prayer

About the Bush: The Five Excuses of Moses
The Five Loves of God
Deepening Our Relationship With Christ
Really Good News For Today!
A Legacy of Kings - Israel's Chequered History
Minor Prophets: Major Issues!
The Tabernacle - God's House of Shadows
Tribes and Tribulations - Israel's Predicted Personalities
Once Saved, Always Saved - The Reality of Eternal Security
After God's Own Heart : The Life of David
Jesus: What Does the Bible Really Say?
God: His Glory, His Building, His Son
The Feasts of Jehovah in One Hour
Knowing God - Reflections on Psalm 23
Praying with Paul
Get Real ... Living Every Day as an Authentic Follower of Christ
A Crisis of Identity
Double Vision: Hidden Meanings in the Prophecy of Isaiah
Samson: A Type of Christ
Great Spiritual Movements
Take Your Mark's Gospel
Total Conviction - 4 Things God Wants You To Be Fully Convinced About
Esther: A Date With Destiny
Experiencing God in Ephesians
James - Epistle of Straw?
The Supremacy of Christ
The Visions of Zechariah
Encounters at the Cross

Five Sacred Solos - The Truths That the Reformation Recovered
Kingdom of God: Past, Present or Future?
Overcoming Objections to Christian Faith
Stronger Than the Storm - The Last Words of Jesus
Fencepost Turtles - People Placed by God
Five Woman and a Baby - The Genealogy of Jesus
Pure Milk - Nurturing New Life in Jesus
Jesus: Son Over God's House
Salt and the Sacrifice of Christ
The Glory of God
The Way: Being a New Testament Disciple
Power Outage - Christianity Unplugged
Windows to Faith: Insights for the Inquisitive

About the Author

Born and educated in Scotland, Brian worked as a government scientist until God called him into full-time Christian ministry on behalf of the Churches of God (www.churchesofgod.info). His voice has been heard on Search For Truth radio broadcasts for over 30 years (visit www.searchfortruth.podbean.com) during which time he has been an itinerant Bible teacher throughout the UK and Canada. His evangelical and missionary work outside the UK is primarily in Belgium and The Philippines. He is married to Rosemary, with a son and daughter.

About the Publisher

Hayes Press (www.hayespress.org) is a registered charity in the United Kingdom, whose primary mission is to disseminate the Word of God, mainly through literature. It is one of the largest distributors of gospel tracts and leaflets in the United Kingdom, with over 100 titles and hundreds of thousands despatched annually. In addition to paperbacks and eBooks, Hayes Press also publishes Plus Eagles Wings, a fun and educational Bible magazine for children, and Golden Bells, a popular daily Bible reading calendar in wall or desk formats. Also available are over 100 Bibles in many different versions, shapes and sizes, Bible text posters and much more!

www.ingramcontent.com/pod-product-compliance
Lightning Source LLC
Chambersburg PA
CBHW031401040426
42444CB00005B/375